Start Your Business in 7 Days

James Caan is one of the UK's most successful and dynamic entrepreneurs, and has been building and selling businesses since 1985.

After dropping out of school at sixteen and starting his first business in a Pall Mall broom cupboard, armed with little more than charm and his father's advice, Caan went on to make his fortune in the recruitment industry, founding the Alexander Mann Group, which grew to a turnover of £130 million. He also co-founded executive headhunting firm Humana International, growing it to 147 offices across thirty countries in six years.

Caan graduated from Harvard Business School in 2003, and went on to set up private equity firm Hamilton Bradshaw. Based in Mayfair, Hamilton Bradshaw specializes in buyouts, venture capital and turnarounds in the recruitment sector, as well as real estate investments and development opportunities in both the UK and Europe.

A winner of PriceWaterhouseCoopers Entrepreneur of the Year and BT Enterprise of the Year awards, Caan joined the panel of the BBC's *Dragons' Den* in 2007. He is a regular in the national and business press, he advises various government programmes, and he initiates philanthropic projects via the James Caan Foundation.

James Caan is the author of *Get the Job You Really Want*, which is also published by Portfolio Penguin.

By the same author

Get the Job You Really Want

Get the Life You Really Want (Quick Reads)

Start Your Business in 7 Days

James Caan

PORTFOLIO
PENGUIN

PORTFOLIO PENGUIN

Published by the Penguin Group
Penguin Books Ltd, 80 Strand, London WC2R ORL, England
Penguin Group (USA) Inc., 375 Hudson Street, New York, New York 10014, USA
Penguin Group (Canada), 90 Eglinton Avenue East, Suite 700, Toronto, Ontario, Canada M4P 2Y3
(a division of Pearson Penguin Canada Inc.)
Penguin Ireland, 25 St Stephen's Green, Dublin 2, Ireland
(a division of Penguin Books Ltd)
Penguin Group (Australia), 250 Camberwell Road, Camberwell, Victoria 3124, Australia
(a division of Pearson Australia Group Pty Ltd)
Penguin Books India Pvt Ltd, 11 Community Centre, Panchsheel Park, New Delhi – 110 017, India
Penguin Group (NZ), 67 Apollo Drive, Rosedale, North Shore 0632, New Zealand
(a division of Pearson New Zealand Ltd)
Penguin Books (South Africa) (Pty) Ltd, 24 Sturdee Avenue, Rosebank, Johannesburg 2196, South Africa

Penguin Books Ltd, Registered Offices: 80 Strand, London WC2R ORL, England

www.penguin.com

First published 2012
002

Copyright © James Caan, 2012
All rights reserved

The moral right of the author has been asserted

Set in TheMix and Trade Gothic
Designed and typeset by Richard Marston
Printed in Great Britain by Clays Ltd, St Ives plc

Except in the United States of America, this book is sold subject
to the condition that it shall not, by way of trade or otherwise, be lent,
re-sold, hired out, or otherwise circulated without the publisher's
prior consent in any form of binding or cover other than that in
which it is published and without a similar condition including this
condition being imposed on the subsequent purchaser

ISBN 978-0-670-92064-8

www.greenpenguin.co.uk

Penguin Books is committed to a sustainable
future for our business, our readers and our planet.
This book is made from Forest Stewardship
Council™ certified paper.

'Your first idea does not have to be your best idea. It is only your first idea. Concentrate on finding the right idea.'

Contents

Introduction

These days, it seems, everybody wants to be an entrepreneur. Perhaps that's down to the challenging state of the job market, or because being an entrepreneur seems to offer a way to control your own destiny in recessionary times. I am acutely aware of this because every day of my life I am bombarded by people who want to set up their own business. I find myself sitting through every kind of presentation and pitch you can imagine.

That's part and parcel of what I do for a living, of course, running my private equity company, Hamilton Bradshaw. And thanks to my time on *Dragons' Den*, it's only natural that many people who believe that they have unearthed the next great business idea might want to run it past me. But I have definitely noticed a significant increase over the past couple of years, not only in the number of approaches, but also in the sheer level of imagination and persistence that these would-be entrepreneurs will use to try to reach me.

The other day I was held up in a traffic jam on the M1. The guy in the car ahead of me recognized my personalized number plate. He opened his door, got out, calmly walked back along the outside lane of the motorway and knocked on my window. I was freaked out.

I lowered the window and he said, 'James, I can't believe I've had this opportunity of meeting you. I was watching your car in my rear-view mirror and realized it must be you.' He went on, 'I've got this idea that I've been working on – and here's my business plan!' To my shock and horror he was carrying a proposal and a sample of his product around with him. I thought, Un*believable*.

Another weekend I was doing a piece for Sky News about the government giving grants to encourage entrepreneurs. It was one of those interviews where the journalist and I were being filmed walking down a street in London chatting to each other. Right in the middle of our conversation a passer-by in a suit stopped me and said, 'Really sorry to interrupt you, James, but I've just read that you have set up a new property company. I've got this amazing penthouse in the West End, and I'm looking for some investment. It's a unique opportunity.' Because I was in the middle of the interview I thought I'd better just give him a card and hope that would deal with it. A couple of days later he texted me: 'Just wanted to let you know, I've got all the information, I'll be sending it across next week, love to follow it up with you . . .'

I get accosted in restaurants, buttonholed at events. People turn up at Hamilton Bradshaw and tell reception, 'I've got a sample I want to leave for James.' I've even had someone ring up and say, 'Hi, could I speak to James? It's his brother calling.' The call got put through. 'Hello, can I help you?' And reception said, 'James, it's your brother on the line.' So I answered, 'Hi, mate, how's it going?' 'Oh hello, James, I just wanted to introduce myself . . .'

I admire their inventiveness, that perseverance and determination. It's great to have such drive and self-belief, and the desire to create something from nothing. It's the same mixture of drive, self-belief and desire that has always fuelled my career.

But – and it's a considerable 'but' – despite all that energy, many, if not most, of these business ideas are destined to go absolutely nowhere. The pitches can range from the fastidiously researched to the totally impromptu, the inspired to the frankly delusional. And often the person pitching to me is so convinced of the brilliance of their new business that they have failed to ask themselves the simplest of questions that could – and should – have saved them expending vast amounts of time and money developing an idea that they should never have pursued. It's something that breaks my heart. In the Den I saw hundreds of people who had lost everything to arrive at the same conclusion that we five Dragons were able to reach in no more than twenty minutes.

Now, of course, I would like to encourage everyone to feel that they can start up their own business. I am a born entrepreneur. I love the thrill of it all, the excitement of the challenges and the problem-solving. It's what gets me out of bed in the morning.

But I also want to go against the grain a little bit. Rather than writing a book that is purely motivational and which promises everything is easy, I want to take a bold step and be realistic. So as well as showing you the route to potential success, I also want to liberate you in a different way, freeing you up from the fear of making mistakes and helping you avoid the possibility of wasting an enormous amount of your own time and money.

That's what this book is all about. I am going to show you how to spend a maximum of seven days deciding if your idea is workable, whether it is bankable. My whole objective is to explain the thought processes that I go through every time I look at a new investment opportunity, to lay out the often very tough questions that you have to ask yourself each step of the way. I want you to become your own Dragon, to be able to say 'I'm in', but equally importantly, to have the courage to say 'I'm out'.

Why seven days? Well, if you believe that God created the world in seven days, setting up a business really shouldn't take that long ... Just kidding. The serious point is that a specific time period will give you a framework for pacing yourself and structuring your key decisions, with a clear set of targets so that you start putting your ideas into action. It is very easy to sit around talking about what you want to do, because at that point the idea is still perfect. By following the stages in this book you will be able to overcome any inertia and start moving forward.

By the end of the seven days, you may come to the conclusion that your idea does have real commercial potential: and that will be fantastic. I'll be delighted.

But equally, when those seven days are over, if not before, you may also decide that your idea is simply not going to be profitable (and remember, your first idea is rarely going to be your best idea). To me that is not a failure, that is a victory, a real result, because it will save you so much in so many ways and allow you to learn from the experience and move on to another idea, which may be the one that works for you.

I take this very seriously, because I know that getting it wrong can be a life-changing experience. One day a woman in her sixties walked into the Den. She was very polished and well dressed. She had been working for the same company for forty years, had taken retirement and received a golden handshake of £250,000. Because she was quite smart, she decided that rather than pop on her slippers just yet, she would start her own business. She pitched us the idea: the concept was very good, but commercially it was simply not viable.

She had already been working on this idea for eighteen months and had spent the entire quarter of a million, blown the lot. Appearing on *Dragons' Den* was her final roll of the dice, and her appearance only proved that her idea was not going to work. If she had come to me on the day she had been given the cheque and said, 'James, I'm about to start my own business and I've come up with this idea,' I could have taken her through each stage of this book, got her to ask herself the right questions, and she would have declared herself out, would still have the £250,000, and would be now enjoying a comfortable retirement. Regrettably, she did none of those things. She didn't ask the questions and so the rest of her life took a huge turn for the worse.

Over the years I have observed that maybe 95 per cent of people – and I'm talking about very experienced, sophisticated businessmen and women, not just the novices and the kids – make the same old mistakes over and over and over again because they don't know any better. Believe me, I have made all those mistakes too – but I have always tried to learn from them. When you've set up as many businesses as I have, when you've got as many wrong as I have, when you've seen so many that have failed, but also so many that have succeeded, you learn how to drill down to the core issues a lot quicker. It's a matter of business survival. I don't see that as a negative but a huge positive.

This book could easily save you thousands of pounds and prevent you wasting months or years of your time. I'm not going to take the decisions or make the hard choices for you, but I will give you the ammunition to help you think for yourself and make the decision that is right for you.

Every day of my life as an entrepreneur I realize that the secret of success is not to act recklessly but the opposite: to minimize risk. So by understanding how to release yourself from unnecessary risk, you will be able to enjoy the exhilaration of the journey even more.

Each piece of advice in this book is based on what I have learnt during the thirty years or so I have been setting up and starting businesses. You will find all the fundamental ingredients for any new company, whatever sector you want to be in, whatever size of business you have in mind, along with the tools, the levers and the key decisions to make it work.

After you have answered all the questions I am going to get you to ask yourself, you will have a business that is worth investing your energy and resources in, and that genuinely has a chance of success. You can be one of the 10 per cent of businesses that do make it.

Now all I need is seven days of your time . . .

Start Your Business in 7 Days

'Before you embark on this exhilerating but daunting journey I want you to take a good, long look at yourself. Do you really, really have what it takes to be an entrepreneur? I call this the Power of Why.'

First Things First: Is This Really Me?

The first question to ask yourself before you start out is a tough one. It's the one question you don't want to ask at the very point you are fired up by the idea of starting your own business. But this is precisely the right moment to take a pause and be honest with yourself about whether you have the determination, the hunger, the DNA of an entrepreneur.

There are shelfloads of books out there that will happily feed your dream, tell you that yes, you too can make a million, a billion, live the lifestyle you are dreaming of, be the next Richard Branson, the next Michelle Mone, the next Innocent smoothie company . . . And there are many benefits: the buzz of setting yourself free, of releasing yourself to make your own decisions, of controlling your own destiny, of saying goodbye to your previous life as Mr or Mrs Robot.

Yet I believe that the only way you can genuinely start following that path is by being calm, clear-headed and rational throughout the process. Yes, demonstrate plenty of enthusiasm and passion, but be prepared to think in a businesslike way at every stage.

As you will find me saying regularly throughout this book, if you look at starting your own business with the right attitude, but find that your first idea, or your first ten ideas, are just not viable, and that you have to say to yourself 'I'm out', that in itself is a hugely positive achievement.

By the end of this chapter, I need you to be certain in your own mind that – despite the allure of being an entrepreneur, and all the temptations of the possible financial upside and the freedom it can offer – you genuinely have what it takes to be an entrepreneur.

I recently did a deal with somebody who typically I *wouldn't* have backed. Alia approached Hamilton Bradshaw with a proposal for a specialist media recruitment consultancy. She was relatively young, but she told me she felt confident that she could deliver.

I met Alia and went through her CV. I could see nothing glaringly obvious in her career so far to suggest that she was capable of setting up and running that kind of business; her CV didn't read any different from that of an experienced recruiter. Nonetheless she had incredible drive and determination, and so I found myself spending quite a lot of time working on her proposal because I sensed she might have that entrepreneurial X-factor, the necessary driving force. She was the youngest of five children, her parents were not particularly well off, and I think she felt she had something to prove, in the way that younger siblings can feel that they've grown up in the hand-me-down category. She was certainly saying all the right things: 'I'm prepared to do whatever it takes. I'm willing to work seven days a week. I'm ready to learn.'

I recommended a set of DVDs from the States on how to become a really effective recruitment consultant. I suggested she watch the whole course and get back to me to tell me what she had learnt. She came in a couple of weeks later and I was blown away by how far she had progressed and how well she had absorbed the lessons from the DVDs – she was virtually reciting whole chapters word for word.

I knew there were hours and hours of footage to watch. So I asked Alia how she had managed to do it. She said, 'The day after I met you I resigned from my job, and since then I've been at home every day studying this material.'

I was taken aback, and quite guilty that she had resigned from her job. I felt that was the last thing she should have done. 'I thought you'd wait until we'd agreed whether we're going to do this or not, whether we're going to make the investment,' I said. She replied, 'I really thought about it, James, and I decided I need to demonstrate to you that I can do this. I don't want to be second-best, and I know you are going to judge me on what I deliver.' She was absolutely right. The message that sent out to me was that here was somebody who was prepared to do whatever it takes.

I gave her a different task, then another. On each one she exceeded my expectations by going that one extra step. For example I told her that one of the elements that would be really important was developing a website for her business, and understanding the identity and branding of it. Shortly afterwards she sent me a PowerPoint presentation in which she had analysed twenty of the competitors in her sector of the market, using screen grabs from all their websites annotated with her comments: 'This is excellent. We don't need that. I like this scheme. This concept would work.' She then took the best of each of those ideas and said, 'This is what my proposition would look like.' I flicked through it and thought to myself, *This is phenomenal.*

I found myself being drawn into the process because Alia never failed at any task. In a funny way I almost wanted to turn down the deal, since in practical terms it was still high risk. There are situations like that where sometimes the theoretical checklist is telling you not to carry on, but every now and then you have to look beyond that and say, 'Does this person really have what it takes?' And I began to believe that she probably did.

She went off, researched the core members of the team she needed, and came back to me with a team who had collectively billed £1 million in the previous year. Not only had she comprehensively inverted my risk, she had categorically proved she had what it took.

Ultimately we go back to the same principle. It's about people. Business is about people who are driven, who are smart, who are streetwise, who are commercial and are prepared to swim that extra mile.

Alia had given me the impression that she was a bit fearless, something that I believe you have to be in business, because you can sit there analysing everything and spending far too long cogitating about whether you should or shouldn't do something, and in the meantime the commercial opportunity has moved on. Fearless people seize the moment.

Crossing the pain threshold

How many entrepreneurs start businesses that *don't* make it? Figures from Companies House showed that between March 2009 and March 2010, over 360,000 businesses were registered, but in the same period about 500,000 enterprises failed. That was the first time in recent history that more companies failed than were registered.

And the ratio between businesses that make it and business *ideas* that fail before they reach the point of being registered is much higher: we never hear about them for the very reason they never get off the ground. I think we could be talking 100:1 in terms of the ratio between failure and success, maybe even as high as 1,000:1.

Now ask yourself: **What is the price you are prepared to pay? What is your personal pain threshold?**

That is why this chapter, before you even set out on the journey, is really important. Look at anyone who has been successful – whether that's Bill Gates, Philip Green, Martha Lane Fox, whichever role model you want to choose. People who want to make it are driven for a reason. And there are many different reasons. The 'Power of Why' can be fuelled by a whole host of issues. But it has to have deep meaning. Otherwise your tolerance level for all the pain, rejection and failure that is going to come your way will not be high enough. Your need to succeed, your 'Why' has to be very strong.

Because I can guarantee that during the course of starting your own business everything that can go wrong *will* go wrong. You'll run out of money, you'll run out of customers, you'll be rejected, you won't win a deal, you won't be able to hire someone you really want, or if you do hire them, they'll leave just when you can least afford to lose them. It's not going to come easy. It is never a walk in the park.

When that inevitable rejection comes, will you be able to say to yourself, 'I really want to get up and fight another day?' Because if you don't have the will to fight, if you don't actually need to fight, the truth of the matter is you won't.

Everybody is unique, of course, and the Why that is driving you could be completely different from the Why for me.

My family came to London from Pakistan in the 1960s. At the time Pakistan's circumstances were such that the country had gone through partition, the economy was on its knees, regular jobs were simply not readily available. Consequently tens of thousands of people emigrated to Canada, America, Australia and the UK. My parents came to Britain for no other purpose than to provide a better life for their family.

When my father arrived here, he couldn't speak, read or write English. He was almost doomed to fail before he started because the odds on him making it were so slim. You can imagine the drive and determination he must have possessed to succeed from that starting point. As a child I grew up in an environment where I saw my parents determined and motivated, my father up and out to work at seven o'clock every morning, rarely getting back home before eleven at night, working on Saturdays and Sundays, doing everything possible to overcome those odds stacked against him.

Consequently, as a family we had hardly any holidays, no real quality of life, and not much fun, to be honest, because my parents were never there: they were only ever out working. I suspect most people these days would consider the price of that success to be too high, and would not be prepared to sacrifice all the things they enjoy. But my father's pain threshold was very high, and the price he was ultimately prepared to pay was even higher, since I believe that he was never really able to enjoy the fruits of his labour. His example gave me an expectation, a mindset, of what I needed to do and how I needed to do it. I think that's the base subconscious in me.

Then the circumstances of my life changed when I took the decision not to join the family business. It must have broken my father's heart. He had worked for fifteen years desperately trying to build a successful leather-goods business, driven by the idea that his sons would come in and take over. And what do I go and do? The worst possible thing I could do, by telling him, 'Sorry, Dad, this isn't for me.'

By doing that I really increased the pressure on myself to succeed, because – given my relationship with my father, and having disappointed him so deeply – I absolutely had to prove to him that I was worthy of his affection. I had to show him that I had made the right decision.

I couldn't go back in a year or two and say, 'You know what, I threw everything back in your face, I didn't go into the family business and, by the way, look at me: I'm a loser.' Nobody ever wants to be placed in that 'I told you so' box. So, having left, I *had* to make it. Imagine how high my pain threshold was as a result; imagine what I would have done to succeed. And that is exactly what I did. I was relentless.

I tell that story because it is so easy to succumb to the dream of future success but not be prepared to pay the dues. If you look too far ahead, and start planning exactly how you'll spend your money, which house, which car, which yacht you'd like to have, you will lose sight of the essentials.

I don't think J. K. Rowling sat down to write a book believing that she would become the world's biggest-selling author. She wrote a book that she really liked, a book that she wanted to sell. Did the Beatles, when they were playing in the Cavern in Liverpool, think for one minute they were going to be the world's greatest band? Of course not.

For the guy who starts a sandwich bar, the fact is he may end up running an operation the size of Pret A Manger, but he doesn't start off believing that. That bit is hype. And worse, that dream is not enough to overcome the first hurdle.

When a dreamer is on the phone trying to sell a product or a service, and the first ten people tell him, 'I'm not interested,' he'll say, 'This is far too hard,' and give up. The other guy, the one who is driven by something much deeper, will come back in the morning, start his working day a little earlier, go in a bit more psyched up. I'm not saying that guarantees he is going to make it, but he will go further, he will push himself harder. That's no different from the analogy of sport: tennis, golf, swimming or cycling, it's the constant, long hours of practice that pay off. No pain, no gain.

The JC twist

When I am recruiting for a position one of my favourite lines to ask is, 'If you had a magic wand and you could do any job you wanted to do, if you could write your own spec, what would it be?' Because if you have another opportunity that better suits their style and their personality, that gets the best from them, a position where they add the greatest value to the company, that is the job they should be doing. Common sense, when you think about it, will tell you they will do really well. The same is true of being an entrepreneur. If you wrote your ideal job spec, would it describe setting up your own business, taking on board all the decisions, all the risk, all the pain – or in fact does the very thought terrify you? Ask the question now, and if you decide you don't want the pain, you might actually be relieved. Better to know that now than when the bank is busy repossessing your house.

Whenever I am considering a business opportunity, I am looking for talented, determined people to work with. The kind of people who, as soon as you meet them, inspire you. You see them and think, *Really bright, really smart, really driven, looks the part, sounds the part.* My objective then is to understand them. Who are you? What are you made of? What is your DNA? What drives you?

In my years working in the recruitment industry, interviewing some of the smartest men and women around, I saw at first hand how important people were to the success, or otherwise, of a business. And I have always been passionate about investing in people, often more than in the idea. I back the person.

When Sammy French came into *Dragons' Den* and I backed her dog treadmill, the product was not what sold the idea to me. I didn't know the market she was involved in, and when she said that she was selling the treadmill for £1,700, it felt to me that all the dynamics of her business were wrong. I didn't really get the idea, the price seemed too expensive, and I wasn't sure how big the market really was. If I had evaluated her proposal purely on the basis of ticking the necessary boxes, especially in the twenty minutes I had available, then the deal would never have happened.

But I looked at the person who was presenting, I listened to what she was saying and I asked her one simple question: 'Sammy, why are you doing this?' She said, 'I come from a pretty good middle-class background, my family did quite well, I went to a good school and got into university. And now I'm a single parent, I've got two kids to bring up and I live in a council flat. One of my daughters is really bright, and I happen to think she would really excel at a private school. But paying the school fees with my income isn't possible. I've taken an extra job, working in a pub, and in the evenings I'm selling these dog treadmills online. If I could get my daughter into a private school, I think I'd be giving her a great start.'

Now think about the Power of Why. The things you would do to give your child a better start in life. The price you would pay for that and the sacrifices you would be prepared to make. Let's imagine somebody called John who has a similar proposal: he's in a good job, he's doing OK and he fancies starting his own business because he wants to make a bit more money. Although John and Sammy both start off on similar journeys, John will probably fall at the first or second hurdle, because his conviction is superficial and the destination he has in mind would be a nice-to-have, not a necessity.

Sammy, on the other hand, will face the same hurdles but subconsciously remind herself that her business, Fit Fur Life, is not about her, not about money, but is about her daughter's future. That is a far stronger driver than the things motivating John, who wants a bigger house, a sleeker car, a better lifestyle. But if he doesn't get any one of those it won't be the end of the world. He won't have a convertible, but he has got a decent saloon already. His house is not detached, but it's a semi in a good location.

So when I look at the Why, as an investor, my only concern is about my level of risk. What I am always trying to do is to work out which is a better risk for me. If I'm going to part with my cash, like anyone I want the highest return for the lowest risk.

Is that going to be John or Sammy? I don't know who will

actually succeed. Both are risks. All I've got to be able to do is evaluate that risk. I backed Sammy – and she made it. The reason I chose her didn't have anything to do with me thinking the dog treadmill was the most ingenious idea in the world. In fact, I thought it was overpriced, and that she was aiming at a really small market. No, the reason I chose her was her.

That's how important you are to your own business. And another vital question to ask, once you have the business idea in mind is, **Am I actually cut out to make a go of this brilliant business idea I've just had?**

Imagine that you have popped into your local café to have a latte and a flapjack. The place is buzzing, there is a fantastic, lively atmosphere. The café is clearly doing really well. You're sitting there and you think to yourself, *God, I bet these people make a lot of money.* I've come across this situation a hundred times, including with my own daughter! 'Dad, let's open a café . . .'

What you then have to do is identify the characteristics of a successful café owner. For a café to do well requires a real people-orientated person in charge, because the entire business is based on interacting with other people, the customers. I don't want to go into a faceless, characterless café on my way to work. I want a place I can walk into where the owner straightaway says, 'Morning, James, same coffee as yesterday?' Then I'm going to feel very special. It requires a certain type of person to run a café. Question: Are you a people person? Because if you are not, then that business isn't really you.

Next, ask yourself what the dynamics of that business are.

The dynamics of a café business include getting up every day at some ungodly hour like five o'clock in the morning. Café-style businesses generally kick off at seven, which means you've got to be there before six, get the bread in and buttered and so on. There are many people I know who are definitely *not* morning people. It doesn't make them good or bad. They're simply not great first thing in the morning.

Of course, you can hire in somebody to run the business for you, who doesn't mind getting up at five o'clock, but – and it is an important 'but' – that is a risk for you because, clearly, they will not have the same drive, determination, commitment and passion as you. For them, it will simply be a job. They will be on a salary. They will never be you. They will not be prepared to go through the pain barriers ahead. And as an investor, if I am considering backing you, if you find somebody to run the café from the start, to me you are far less credible than if you were in there making it happen.

Also, the café business is all about very small transactions – three to five pounds a pop. Again, is that you? Because maybe you're a graduate with an economics degree, and you would be better suited to dealing with much larger transactions. Running a café demands a certain way of buying, of controlling stock. You have to deal with the principle of perishables and non-perishables. The business is very staff-intensive – and that might be an issue, because entrepreneurs are not automatically great managers of people, and in a café managing staff who are generally on minimum or just above minimum wage is a skill in itself.

You need to compare your strengths to your business idea. Are you an indoors or outdoors kind of person? Are you used to getting your hands dirty or do you need a pristine environment to function properly? Do you enjoy travelling a lot, or do you want to spend as much time as possible close to home? Understanding your own personality will help you to determine the business idea that will work for you.

Are age and experience relevant?

While I was assessing the prospect of setting up the recruitment business that Alia, in her mid-twenties, was proposing, one of my main concerns was that she might be too young. Then I realized that I had set up my first business at almost exactly the same age.

I am obviously a lot older now and far more experienced. I recognize and I know what's involved in starting your own business. And the world has moved on in the past twenty-five years. There are far more complexities and procedures, many more regulations, a tangled web of red tape that can stifle a young business: VAT, PAYE, employment law, health and safety, accounting, statutory accounts. Starting up from scratch is not as easy as it was in my early days.

If I have got somebody sitting in front of me who says, 'Look, I've been working for a recruitment business for ten years. Last year I billed £500,000, and by the way here are six people I've worked with in the past who all want to come and join me,' that is a low-risk decision for me. Relevant experience that can be quantified is always going to be a plus point.

At the other end of the spectrum to a twenty-year-old with no experience but bundles of energy and a bright idea might be a fifty-year-old with a huge amount of experience, somebody who has run a large company or a major division, shouldered plenty of responsibility and been really successful. Let's imagine that after thirty years working for other people they now want to step out and set up a recruitment business on their own. They send me a proposal: I look at their CV and it is really impressive.

But then I look at that person and consider the fact that the last time they actually picked up a phone, hired consultants and led by example was probably fifteen years ago. Has too much water gone under the bridge? Could they start again?

I remember when I sold my first business, Alexander Mann, and then started again with a new venture. It was really hard. I had been the group chief executive of a £100-million empire, with 200 people working for me in a huge office. Next thing you know I was walking into a serviced office and it was just me and the *Yellow Pages*. That day I thought to myself, *I remember this. This is hard.*

I had not done any of the basics for years. Three days later somebody rang me up and suggested we go out for lunch. I looked in my pocket; I had no cash. I'd never been to an ATM in my life. I was forty-two years old and I had never used a cashpoint, because I'd never needed to. I was used to giving my

PA my card: she knew my PIN, she'd go and get the cash and it was there when I needed it.

When you are setting up your own business you are going to have to roll your sleeves up and get stuck in. In a normal company there are many different functions and departments. The accounts team sort out the invoices, they get logged on the system, the bills get paid, the VAT and PAYE gets done. The IT team will deal with your software upgrades, syncing your BlackBerry or your iPhone to your computer. You take it all for granted.

A friend of mine who was in the process of setting up his own business said to me, 'I had no idea how to set up my computer. I thought I was just going to pop out to PC World and buy my PC, but, James, they started asking me dozens of questions: how many megs and gigs and this and that, what are you going to use and how much memory? I don't know any of that. All I know is that I used to walk into the office and turn it on. It always worked and if it didn't work, I'd pick up the phone and somebody fixed it. Now I'm sitting there thinking, *Who's going to fix it when it goes wrong? What do I actually do? Who do I call?'*

For somebody who has been really successful, generally working for somebody else, risen through the ranks, the decision to go it alone requires a different level of thought. **In the beginning you are going to spend at least 20 per cent of your time doing stuff that is frankly menial, but the question is, if you're not doing it, who else is going to?** And for the more corporate people that becomes a massive fear factor. You are climbing down a long way.

Also, at that level, what happens is that you underestimate the power of the brand that you work for. One of the biggest challenges that entrepreneurs face is when they have worked for an established business with a strong brand. Let's say you've been working in retail for one of the big brand-name stores. Things have gone really well, customers have been flocking in, people are happy to pay the prices the store charges, and after a while you think, *I'm running a store that generates £1 million a week in sales. If I was to set up by myself, because these are all my customers, I can achieve the same level of sales* and *make more money for myself.*

Off you go and set up on your own, and then to your dismay you discover that those customers weren't really yours, they actually belonged to the brand. They were loyal to the brand before they were loyal to you.

And even if you're working in a service industry, maybe an ad agency or financial services business, sometimes we start to believe in our own publicity. It's only when we leave and we call the customers we used to have that there is a sudden and brutal realization: what am I actually offering these clients? I really am just a start-up. There's no back-up, there's no service, no follow-through, whereas with an established brand you've got all that comfort and security, the expertise, the track record, the database – and you no longer have that to rely on.

For anyone in a corporate job who is tempted to become an entrepreneur, this is one of the biggest questions I would be asking them. **How much of your success was really you? How much was about the company or the brand that you worked for?**

If somebody comes to work for me as an investment manager at Hamilton Bradshaw, they know that the phone will ring. And of course it feels the job is easy. Whereas if you went out and did it yourself you might struggle to find clients. Hamilton Bradshaw is based in an attractive period building in Mayfair, a very prestigious location, tastefully refurbished. There's a sense of establishment whenever somebody comes through the door, a feeling that we have been around, we know who we are. When you take all that away – the brand, the location, the support, the infrastructure – it's never going to be as easy.

So before you start out, weigh up the risks. Being too young, lacking relevant experience or never having run a business before are all high risk factors, but it can be equally high risk at the other end of the scale, only in a different way.

What's interesting is that recently there has been a growth amongst both older people going into entrepreneurship and recent school-leavers and graduates setting up their own businesses, which proves that all these risks can be overcome.

Is it possible to be a part-time entrepreneur?

I meet a lot of people who have full-time jobs who confidently tell me, 'On the side, I'm working on this great idea.' How many of these people have businesses on the side that have really flown? The answer is, very few. And those that did, did so purely by chance.

I personally don't believe in the idea of a part-time entrepreneur. It's a bit like hiring somebody to work three days a week: they never gel within the team, and problems and crises unfortunately tend to occur in the two days they're not there. There's no continuity, there's no consistency. If you put a bit of part-time into a business, you're only going to get a bit of part-time out. You're not going to see it rocket upwards.

That's why it is so important to go through the next seven days of evaluation *before* giving up your day job. When Alia told me she had resigned from her job after one meeting with me, there was nothing I could do about it, but I would never have advised her to do that if she had asked me. What we are talking about is not the action, but the attitude.

The positives of setting up your own business

Freedom, freedom, freedom! Previously you have been a character in somebody else's story. When you work in the same environment, doing the same thing every day, you feel like a cog in the machine. But start your own business and you've just been liberated. Now you are in control of your destiny. You're in control of your life. You can determine whether you start work at 7.15 – but you know what? Maybe it's 9.00, or 10.00. Maybe this morning you're going to work from home.

The JC twist

The quest for freedom, the thrill of making your own choices. That should be exhilarating, shouldn't it? But some people find that prospect frightening. It gives them vertigo. In most staff reviews I do, one of the biggest frustrations employees express is, 'I need more responsibility, I need more autonomy. I need to be able to make my own decisions – this is really frustrating me.' During nearly every review I hear the same script. And when I say, 'OK, tell me what it is you want to do,' what do you think happens? They have no idea. So I say, 'Hang on, I said to you that you can make your own decisions. If you want to pay that bill, pay it. If you want to do that deal, do it.' 'But I don't know . . .' If we are being honest, most of us don't want to think about taking decisions, we want somebody else to think for us. If that is what you feel deep down, if you are not sure you can cope with the prospect of failure or the loneliness of the long-distance entrepreneur, that doesn't reflect badly on you. It's a natural reaction. But it might just mean you are not cut out to be an entrepreneur.

The sense of liberation, of freedom, the sense of being able to craft your own destiny, direct your own journey, is a fantastic feeling. For perhaps the first time in your working life you are in the driving seat, you are no longer a passenger.

For me that automatically unleashes a great feeling of excitement, motivation, drive and ambition. You've been let out of the 'cage'.

So remember the critical question – **Is this really me? Am I ready to take on the highs and lows of being an entrepreneur?**

And give yourself a quick checklist: review your real core motivation, quantify your personal pain threshold, think about the kind of business that best suits your personality and preferences, and consider how your age and practical experience might come into play.

And if the answer is still, 'Yes. I'm in,' well, welcome to the club. Have a good night's sleep, because tomorrow is Day 1.

"Remember that your first idea does not have to be your best idea. It is only your first idea. Don't worry if it's not workable. Move on. Learn from the experience. Concentrate on finding the right idea. The question to ask is not *What is unique about my idea?* but *What is compelling about it?*"

DAY 1:
IS MY IDEA REALLY
A BUSINESS?

You probably have a business idea in mind already. Or maybe you feel you have the instincts of an entrepreneur but haven't yet found an idea that inspires you or feels right for you. My gut feeling is that you are more than likely to fall into the first category, because nine times out of ten the impetus for thinking about setting up a business is the direct result of coming across a problem that needs solving.

It is perfectly possible to approach the question of looking for a new business in a clinical, purely analytical way, but I tend to believe that those ideas which spark genuine enthusiasm and passion from Day 1 are the ones that will give you enough commitment to carry you through all the ups and downs of the process.

The one thing I can't provide you with is that original idea – that's the element you are bringing to this whole process. But what I can do is help you examine the ideas you do have and offer you some perspectives for assessing them and tools for testing them.

The spark of a business idea can come from anywhere, at any time, but the realization that there is a product or a service you need and can't find is one of the most common motivators.

The idea for fashion retailer Next emerged out of the simple observation that people's biggest frustration when clothes shopping is trying to match items. If you're a man, you might go and buy a suit and then find you can't decide which tie goes best with it, or which shirt or shoes. We generally walk around shops rather aimlessly trying to work all this out.

For George Davies, the creator of the concept, whose motto is 'retail is detail', the eureka moment was realizing, 'You know what we should do is put the shirt next to the suit, with the tie next to the shirt, and the socks and shoes underneath – and we'll have done all the thinking for the customer. Because actually we would much rather have somebody else do that for us.' Everything would be next to the items that matched. Customers would come out of the store having bought five items rather than just one. Problem solved: a great, profitable retail idea – and an instant brand name into the bargain.

Liz Earle, who now runs one of the world's top skincare companies, is another classic example: she is quite open about the fact that she used to have bad skin and that her problem was one of the primary reasons for her moving into the skincare sector. As she puts it, 'If you can't find what you want, make it yourself!'

Again one specific, and in this case quite personal, concern inspired a viable, and ultimately very successful, business idea.

What if I haven't found my idea yet?

If you don't yet have a product or service in mind, don't start out by asking, 'What should I do?' It's a natural enough question, but I think it is really hard to answer. Most people end up with a blank. It's the entrepreneur's equivalent of writer's block.

You can try any number of techniques to generate ideas: brainstorming, mindmapping, listmaking, storyboarding, daydreaming. But I think it is much better and more practical to ask, 'What *don't* I want to do?' And by analysing your answers you will find you get a lot closer to what you *do* want to do.

It's just like when you leave school or come out of college and are wondering, 'What job am I going to do?' So many people at that point say, 'Oh, I don't really know.' I understand that. There's nothing unusual about finding yourself in that particular quandary. So what's the solution? I've always found it is much easier to begin with what someone knows – instinctively – they wouldn't be happy doing.

For example I'll say, 'OK, do you want to be a plumber?' 'No.' 'Or would you like to be a firefighter?' 'No, not really.'

These are usually straightforward decisions; they are easily reached and take very little thinking about.

This process is a good one to try out. I've done this for myself many times. And you can keep going along this journey in the same way. 'Right. You don't want to be a firefighter. That's fine. Now tell me why.' Again, **that's the key question, not 'What do you want to do?' but 'Why don't you want to do that?'**

Maybe the main drawback to becoming a firefighter is a fear of heights. 'OK, so you can't do anything where heights is going to be an issue. Write down "heights".' 'Oh, the other reason is because they have to spend too much time outdoors.' 'That's a really big one. You're not really an outdoors kind of person. Write that down too.' 'And there's not enough money in it.' 'So money's really important.'

And as this list of negatives is jotted down, and you start to dig a bit deeper and analyse what lies behind each of them, you find that almost without realizing it you are getting a little closer to what you do want to do, gravitating towards an answer more quickly than if you'd started out with, 'What should I do?' It's a technique that really helps you understand your own motivation.

This career-deciding technique works equally well for generating business ideas. Don't focus on what you do want to do. Start with what you don't want to do. It won't take you that long.

And the truth is that maybe you will find that you end up far closer to home than you expected, in an area you already know well, because many of the best business ideas are essentially improvements on what already exists in the market.

You don't need to come up with a brand-new idea. Go back to your CV and look at what you already know.

The JC twist

When I worked in a shop, there were two particular aspects of the job I disliked intensely. The first was that I had to stand up all day, on my feet almost non-stop from eight or nine in the morning till six, which I found really boring. And secondly I didn't like working on Saturdays; I felt that it affected my social life. I was fully aware of what I did not enjoy about my current job, so when I noticed an advert for a position in a recruitment company, what were the two things that the job offered that really attracted me? They didn't open Saturdays. And I'd be sitting down all day. Just look at how those two fundamental, simple elements made such a difference to me, because by moving into the recruitment business I found the perfect environment for my own first entrepreneurial activities.

Do I need a unique idea?

Being so close to your own idea can easily blind you to a very basic weakness in it. One of the *Dragons' Den* pitches was for a cabinet that turned into an ironing board. My view was that the woman who presented had invented something to solve a problem that didn't exist. At first sight it might seem great, but think about the logistics. First, how many people don't already have an ironing board? Hardly any. And how many people don't already have an iron? Ditto. And how many people don't have some sort of cabinet? Exactly. So she was making some big assumptions: that I, her future potential customer, would be sitting there with none of the above. But she hadn't thought about that because she was focused purely on her invention.

There is very little in business that is truly unique. Somebody else somewhere in the world, on the other side of the globe or just down your street, is having the same idea as you, right now, whatever it is you've come up with as a product or service.

I frequently sit through hour-long presentations, listening to people telling me that their business proposal is a 'unique' idea, and at the end of it all I will turn to them and say, 'You know what, Bob, it is a great idea, but the problem is everybody's doing it. What is it that you have got that you really think is unique in your proposition?' Because whether you want to set up a publishing business, a flower stall, a window-cleaning company or a financial services consultancy, every market is already pretty well saturated, if it is a worthwhile market.

Let's say I decide I want to come up with an airline business tomorrow. Great. What am I offering that is better than the other airlines competing in the marketplace? If I want to travel in fantastic comfort, there are ten existing airlines I can fly with who already offer that. If I want a bargain-price ticket there are another ten airlines I can book with. At every level of service, top end or bargain basement, there's already somebody out there doing it, so what is the difference? As a rule of thumb, unless you can do something quicker, cheaper or better you are not going to be in with a shout. Too often the entrepreneurs I meet have convinced themselves that the one small twist that they've come up with is enough, but usually it's not, it's merely a cosmetic difference masking the fact that they are not offering a real, significant, material improvement.

Let's stick with the airline example. Look at easyJet. What did Stelios Haji-Ioannou do that was so ingenious? When he set up the company, did airlines exist? Yes. Were people flying to Europe? Of course. Was the internet up and running? It was. Every component of the business was already there. He just did it differently, that's all. The fundamental difference was that he decided not to fly a plane with empty seats, unlike British Airways who were prepared to fly half-full, because their mindset was to charge a fixed seat price and that's that. Stelios said, 'Why do that? Why not sell every seat?' And he got someone to devise a computer algorithm that adjusted the ticket prices in real time: if demand was high, the ticket price went up, if demand was low, it came right down to bargain level to guarantee a full plane. If you've ever flown easyJet you'll know the flight is going to be full. Ingenious, simple and brilliant.

Is your idea a business – or is it a hobby?

There are many ideas which at first sight seem to offer a business opportunity, but actually they are just hobbies. Remember, the reason most people come up with an idea is because they are solving a problem.

Your uncle Jeff is out in the garden, doing some shovelling, but he's ricked his back, and as he's standing there he starts thinking to himself, 'There's got to be another way of doing this shovelling. With all this bending my back's killing me. What I really need to be able to do is shovel standing up.' So he shuts himself away for three years in his shed at the bottom of the garden, spending every spare hour he has designing a shovel which will allow him to do this. And because it's solved his problem, Jeff is convinced he has just discovered the new cat's eyes. But the reality is that he has only solved his own problem. His invention is not a business. The vast majority of people would think that he has just come up with a business. And the reason there are so many failures out there is that they have not yet grasped the difference between a business and a hobby.

A hobby is Uncle Jeff and his shovel. And if Uncle Jeff reads this book then, although he might be on the verge of giving up his comfortable £40,000-a-year job to go into business on his own because he's found a shovel that he can use, I want him to realize that it really isn't a business, it is a personal passion.

And if he realizes that, then this book has succeeded. Jeff

can hold on to the job he already has, and enjoy this sideline hobby where every month he is going to produce four shovels out there in his shed, and then sell them to his mates whose backs are also playing up. Lots of people do that; there's nothing wrong with it. I'm not saying that an idea which turns out to be a hobby is good, bad or indifferent. What I am saying is, 'Now that you recognize it is a hobby, you have to make a decision whether to give up the day job or not.' But at least you know what it is you're dealing with.

I encounter this every day of every week, because everyone experiences problems, and lots of people sit there thinking about those problems. There was one guy on *Dragons' Den* who had tried to undo a nut in his sink to get the tap out, which turned out to be something of a drama because he couldn't get the spanner in the tight space. He spent three hours trying to get this nut off, and he thought there must be loads of people who were experiencing the same thing. He devoted months to coming up with some contraption that enabled him to take the nut out. He absolutely believed he had had his personal 'Eureka!' moment. As his contraption undid the nut, his eyes lit up. Already he was envisaging the business that was going to make his fortune. But if he had paused, and defined what he had, he would have said to himself, 'This is not a business because nobody will ever know it exists.'

Let's even give him the benefit of the doubt and say he gets his nut-undoer into B&Q. He's done well to get the order. I'm home one weekend, trying to resolve the problem of the nut under my sink. I'm in my bathroom, the tap's not working. I am getting frustrated trying to undo it, but would I even think that anything other than the obvious spanner even existed? How would I know it even exists? Because B&Q are not going to run a TV commercial for one specialist item. And even if later that day I went into B&Q, walked down one of their aisles, and saw the gadget sitting on a shelf, would I even know what it did? So as I sat there in the Den listening to his pitch, in my mind I was thinking, **There is no business here. He's not going to sell enough for it to be a business.** I said I was out.

I think this principle of hobby versus business is very important. Right now there are thousands of people out there who are about to give up their day job to spend more time on a favourite pastime or personal project, because they have not seen that it's a hobby.

There's a variation on that which I call a 'commercial hobby'. Perhaps you have a small antiques business that you can run online in the evenings and at weekends, or a stall you have at a local market where you take £1,000 and make £300. You are able to turn a small profit to give yourself a little extra pocket money – there's nothing wrong with that, but you are not likely to, and perhaps don't want to, scale it up in size. I think if you described that to most people they would say that is not what we think of as a business, it's a commercial hobby.

What I want to do is help every one of the people looking at a hobby, even a commercial hobby, to understand the reality of what they have. And, therefore, please don't give up the day job. Because that is suicide. But believe me, there are people out there giving up the day job in favour of a hobby, doing it for six to twelve months, losing their shirt and then realizing at the end that they are never going to sell more than six to ten of these shovels or ironing-board-cum-cabinets a month, which will never be enough to replace the income of the job they walked away from. Suddenly that very enjoyable activity turns into something distinctly less enjoyable the moment it becomes the only thing funding your mortgage payments.

Not only that, but time and time again I come across similar situations where entrepreneurs have not accounted for their own time. All those evenings and weekends spent slaving over the idea represent a cost of time. The business equation is simple: the price of whatever item or service you are selling must equal Cost of Goods + Cost of Time + Cost of Opportunity (the money you need to spend to get your customers and supply them) + Profit. If you don't include your cost of time it is a false equation – I'll come back to that point again and again.

Somewhere between a hobby and a business lies the idea that is a lifestyle: you're providing a service that you might be extremely good at, but you can only develop it up to a certain point. You cannot scale yourself out – for example build up the business to the stage where you can franchise it – because the only person who can do what you are doing is you, and there are only so many hours in your life.

Setting up a business which is a lifestyle is a different, deliberate and perfectly acceptable choice. One of the incorrect assumptions that people usually make is that everybody wants to be a multimillionaire. Not everybody does. They think they do, because who wouldn't? It's a bit like you saying, 'I'd love to have a Porsche 911 Carrera.' Of course you would. But you'll still get from A to B in a Mercedes, a Volvo, a Toyota or a Smart car.

The danger lies in setting out with the belief that you are going to be the next Bill Gates, and ending up with a lifestyle operation. If at the outset you thought that you would maybe make £100,000 a year, which could provide you and your family with a good lifestyle, and if you were content with that, then the chances of you achieving your goal are quite realistic.

But if you thought you *were* going to be the next Bill Gates you would never even achieve the lifestyle stage because your decision-making all along the journey would be skewed. You'd reach for the sky and catch nothing. You'd end up stressed, disappointed and frustrated. Whereas if you understood that what you were aiming for was a lifestyle that suited you, the family, the kids, the chances are you could make the lifestyle work, and be satisfied. You have to understand the dynamics.

Getting feedback on your ideas

If I'm appearing at an event, I can guarantee that during the course of the day somebody will come up to me and say – in all seriousness – something along the lines of, 'James, do you think I should start a hotel business?' I don't even know the guy. Never met him, don't know anything about him. What does he really expect me to say? I can't possibly give a meaningful, useful or practical answer.

If you go to your best friend, and say, 'Chris, do you think I should start my own business?' and Chris says, 'Yeah, that's a great idea,' that is not a helpful answer for you to get, unless by pure chance he happens to be in that industry already. Otherwise what he should do is help you by being honest and saying, 'I really don't know.' It's a bit like going into your local surgery and asking the doctor whether you should become an architect. It's not what your GP does. They're not in a position to give you that advice.

The problem is that because Chris is your friend, you are going to hang on to his every word. If he says, 'I think it's a great idea, mate, I think you should definitely go ahead and set up a café,' that is a completely meaningless conversation. But how often do you think it takes place? I think it happens 95 per cent of the time: people plough ahead and set up businesses that are doomed never to work because at some point their nearest and dearest have told them that it's a brilliant idea and they should do it. They proceed on the most limited amount of information, from people who have no knowledge, no experience, no objectivity. The reality is that friends and family generally – not always, of course, but generally – give really bad advice simply because they have no experience in the sector you are thinking of going into.

Let's go back to *Dragons' Den*. Look at the people who have come up with the most extraordinary and impractical ideas: are you really telling me they had never spoken to anybody about that idea? Do you think that a guy who trots up the stairs and pitches his electric cucumber slicer mounted on a tricycle has never talked about his invention with his mates or his mum? And guess what they must have told him? 'Great idea.'

What you desperately need to avoid is building up false hopes about your idea, because it is precisely those artificial and unrealistic hopes that mean you'll get it wrong and fall flat on your face.

Remember that nobody who appears on *Dragons' Den* is any different from you. Every one of those people who walks through the door believes 100 per cent in their product, their invention, their service. The question is, why do they believe in that? I'm telling you, it's because somebody somewhere along the line told them they were great. That's a real injustice.

How do you deal with that? Before you ever ask advice from family or friends you should sit down with them and have a frank conversation. Tell them, 'I'm about to make a big decision. I trust you and I know you. So please don't lie to me. Please, I beg you, don't tell me what you think I want to hear. Tell me what you really believe. And if I ask you a question to which you don't know the answer, just tell me that straight. I won't be offended. Feel free to point me in the right direction, but don't tell me it's a great idea simply to please me.'

Oh, and by the way, the second golden rule of starting up your own business is that an electric cucumber slicer mounted on a tricycle is never going to be a good idea. Trust me on that one.

Part of the skill in being an entrepreneur is a willingness

to seek out feedback, which can be negative, critical, disheartening, although you need to recognize which the useful, honest feedback is. The upside is that sharing your idea with other people will ease the burden. It will liberate you.

You need to engage with other people. Don't undertake this journey entirely on your own. It's a recipe for disaster. Engage with as many people as possible because what will happen is that the journey will define the idea. You will learn that you shouldn't do *this*, but you could do *that*. *This* might not work, but *that* might. Feedback will help you improve, refine and evolve your idea.

Don't be paranoid

Of course, as soon as I suggest that you should share your ideas, everyone starts getting very paranoid. 'But if I tell somebody else, they might nick my idea, and go off and do it themselves.'

Let me tell you why you should not be paranoid. If you really believe that standing in a pub talking with your mate about your idea in a ten-minute conversation means that he's going to nip off next day and replicate it, the question you need to ask yourself is: **How good was the idea? How real is it?** Because what I am hearing is that the idea is not going to happen anyway. You're telling me that you're worried your mate will copy your idea. If that's true, what do you think is going to happen the moment your product appears on the shelf? A factory in China is going to be able to replicate it in about thirty seconds. There were copies of Kate Middleton's wedding dress on sale online within twenty-four hours of the Royal Wedding. If it's that easy to copy, it's not worth doing in the first place.

The JC twist

Rather than being afraid to share your idea I am going to give you completely the opposite advice. I want you to tell as many people as you can, and not only that, push them for constructive feedback. The feedback is the critical element. Let's say you come in and pitch me an idea: 'James, I've got this amazing idea which is going to change the world [and believe me, that's what everybody says], isn't it great?' If all I do is sit there and agree with you, 'Yes, I think your idea is great,' I don't think you've gained anything from me. You've seen no value from the conversation.

My advice to you is (a) to tell as many people as possible but (b) when you've told them don't just ask them whether they think it's great, ask them why they think it won't work. That's a much better question. Because if you ask ten people that question I will guarantee you that one of them will tell you something you had never thought about. And that one thing could make the difference between it succeeding and not.

If I have come up with a great idea, I am very excited, it's my idea, my baby. I probably experienced a problem which inspired me to create or invent this idea. I'm really passionate about it. Then I share it with you. To you it's a good idea, but you don't have the same level of conviction or passion about it because it's not your idea.

Generally speaking I would say that very few people ever rip somebody else's idea off. The percentage is so small that it is immaterial. Now I can't say to you it will *never* happen, but on the balance of probability the likelihood of it happening is not significant.

A fundamental fear in 90 per cent of the people who are out there as potential entrepreneurs is believing that everybody is desperate to steal their idea. I see it whenever they come to me and say, 'I've got this idea, but James, the biggest problem I have is that I've been working on this for a year and I can't really talk to anybody about it because I haven't got it patented.' Worse, they start digging non-disclosure agreements out of their briefcases before they will even tell me what their idea is. I look at them and I sigh to myself because I am thinking, *You don't even know if anybody's going to buy it.*

Don't go to the patent lawyer just yet

One area in which it is very easy to be drawn into expending an enormous amount of time on a business idea – if it's a product – is over the issues of patents. Almost everybody who comes up with a new product idea will run to a patent agent, because that's the psyche, the culture of this country, if you have an idea.

Imagine, for the sake of illustration, that you have come up with a brand-new way of boiling eggs. You've sat there and thought, *The whole world boils an egg in water, so I am going to create an alternative.* It's a brilliant idea: a machine where you stick the egg in; it's battery-operated, doesn't use any water, and in three minutes the egg is boiled to perfection.

You've spent weeks, months, working on ideas, trying to decide whether it should be in plastic or metal, whether it should be mains-powered rather than battery. But you are not even going to think about the logistics of manufacturing, pricing and distribution because you are still paranoid that someone's going to nick your idea of the waterless egg boiler. Before you even talk to anybody else to get some critical, useful feedback, you rush off to the nearest patent lawyer with your plans.

When you sit in his beautifully appointed office, the patent lawyer is not really interested in whether your idea is going to work or not, because his aim is to persuade you to patent the idea. To him you simply represent his next fee. He makes money from producing patents, so he is never going to tell you not to register a patent. Why would he? That's not his job.

He'll ask you, 'Now, how is this egg boiler going to be powered?' and you'll tell him, 'It uses batteries.' Great, and he'll patent it with the batteries. The fact that I could create exactly the same egg boiler as yours with an electric mains power source is of no interest to him. He won't say to you, 'You do realize, don't you, that if somebody turns that into a mains-operated one, your patent is invalid?' All he will do is what you tell him to do, which is to patent what you have got.

I remember somebody came into the Den with a garment idea, and he told us, 'I've patented this.' We all looked at him and said, 'What?' Because with a garment idea you can patent the garment in that fabric, but all I've got to do is change the fabric and I can copy it. So many people don't spend the time asking the critical question about the value of the patent they have acquired: what does it prevent?

Let me tell you what I would do. First of all, I wouldn't bother with a patent, because my attitude would be, 'Let's assume you can produce it, let's assume you can find somebody to manufacture it, roughly what is it going to cost?' And if the answer is £25 then straightaway I can tell you that your egg boiler, however brilliantly conceived, however sleekly designed, however 'unique', is not going to work, because it is too expensive an alternative to a simple saucepan and that means I am not even going to bother patenting it.

But even if I did think there was something worth patenting, my next question would be, **'What would somebody have to do to create something as close as possible to what I've got without breaching the patent?'**
You would be amazed at the response you would get. I guarantee you that 90 per cent of those people have never asked that question. And had they done so they would have realized the value of the patent is negligible.

Take your precious, expensively acquired patent to some

other patent lawyer and say, 'I have a similar idea to this. What could I do to make my product out of patent?' and to your astonishment it will take him less than ten minutes. He'll say, 'All you have to do is move this bit here up two inches and you've not infringed the patent.' Or, 'Their patent is in plastic, James, so why don't you use a chrome finish?' It really is that simple. How many people understand that? Very few. Because they don't ask the question. Every time I have done it, I've had the answer in ten minutes.

Yet the average entrepreneur is going to waste up to a year trying to patent their idea, and spend ten grand, absolute minimum, on the patenting process. At the end of all that effort to get their patent, they will spend another six months working out the logistics of design, production, prototypes, manufacture, the distribution, all the rest of it. And generally by then they've spent everything they have. It's human nature: whatever they've got they spend. Only to find it doesn't work.

The power of ideas

If by now you have come to the conclusion that your first idea is not a business, appreciate what you have achieved. Relish your decision, because you could have wasted a year, and all your savings, and come up with nothing, but together we have been able to prevent you losing your job, your money, your happiness.

A theme I constantly come across in books and articles aimed at entrepreneurs is 'Whatever you do, never give up'.

I am giving you a different message. **Don't be frightened of giving up on the wrong idea.** That is the opposite to most advice. Whenever somebody came into the Den, even as it was clear every Dragon was going to say 'I'm out', when we asked them, 'In the event you don't get an investment today, what will you do?' they all said, 'We are going to carry on.'

If you have one idea you can have another. Your first idea is part of the journey of finding the right idea. Too many people come up with one idea, discover that particular idea is not going to work and declare, 'Therefore I am not an entrepreneur.' That is not the correct conclusion.

That's like a salesperson saying, 'I've called a buyer, pitched the idea, she's not interested, therefore I should give up.' No. What we are taught in sales is that every 'no' you get is one step closer to getting a 'yes'.

Now go back to the question for Day 1: Is your idea really a business? Check that the idea you have generated is one you can feel passionate about and committed to, but don't fall so in love with it that you are blinded to any weaknesses. Analyse it and define what the compelling selling point of it is. Determine whether it is a hobby, a commercial hobby, a lifestyle or a scalable business idea, and decide whether that is what you want. Share your idea to get feedback and improve it.

And again, remember that every idea you have that doesn't work is one idea closer to the right one, provided you are determined to be an entrepreneur. When you come up with an idea you have to accept and understand that **success is not about the idea, it is about you**.

'Today we are going to take your idea and give it a good workout, get you to test it, push it and stretch it to see if the idea stands up to some basic scrutiny.'

DAY 2:
DOES MY IDEA WORK?

Day 1 is over. And you're still in.

You've convinced yourself that you are made of the right stuff to be an entrepreneur. I applaud that. And you have made sure that your first idea has more substance than some harmless diversion, a pleasant hobby to occupy you on wet weekend afternoons, that it is something with at least the potential to become a meaningful business. Great.

Now it is time to start asking the most critical question that a Dragon would instinctively be thinking about. Put simply, will your idea work?

During any one series of *Dragons' Den*, we filmed on average for six weeks, five working days a week. And during the course of each of those thirty days we would see seven pitches, a total of 210 pitches each series. I was a Dragon for four series of the show, so in *Dragons' Den* alone I saw over 800 pitches. And I've probably sat through somewhere in the region of another 1,200 since setting up Hamilton Bradshaw.

So the criteria I want you to have in mind, the thinking you should be going through, the questions you will bring to bear on your idea, all of that represents the distillation of my experience of considering and analysing every single presentation by those 2,000-plus entrepreneurs who have pitched me their idea. Condensed down into the seven days of this book, I believe this could actually save you a fortune. And I use the word 'fortune' deliberately, because it is all relative. For you £100,000 may represent a fortune. For the next guy £20,000 is a fortune, because that is all he's got.

I was in a black cab once and I heard on the radio that Paul McCartney had just donated £1 million to a charitable organization. I was sitting there thinking, *Very good, Paul. I take my hat off to you.* And do you know what the cab driver said? He muttered, 'Tight bastard.' He was obviously thinking that if you have £500 million and you're only giving £1 million away, it's nothing. My view was completely opposite, that giving £1 million to charity takes something special, I don't care how much you earn. It's funny how people's minds work.

Now, if you take a step back and look at the *Dragons' Den* process without emotion, the reality is that here are five very experienced, intelligent business people who have come into the Den, prepared to spend their own cash, looking for investments, and within twenty minutes those five people have listened to your presentation, analysed your business and given you a reasoned response – 'I'm in', or more often than not, 'I'm out'.

And yet whenever we explained our reasons for not making

an investment, how many times did the person who was pitching to us say they were going to soldier on regardless? As I sat there I knew that, sadly, they really would continue while they still had any money left and that they would carry on until they ran out of cash and only then, only when there was nothing else left, would they put their hands up and quit.

Why would you want to lose everything you own?

Of course, the Dragons are not infallible. If everything in business was guaranteed, there would be no risk to take, and the predictability would remove the buzz that is the fun and challenge of being in business. The classic example is the Trunki kids' suitcase, which none of us decided to invest in and which went on to be a huge success.

Most people who come up with an idea can find somebody who will be able to give them a back-of-an-envelope indication of its viability as a new business. I can ask half a dozen questions and get a feel for the essentials of a proposal, whatever that idea is. The numbers I gather in answer to those questions might be out by 15 to 20 per cent, but they will always provide me with a good benchmark. The precise costs are never going to be the deal breaker. Just give me a range and I will take a view.

For an inexperienced entrepreneur the natural tendency is to spend three months getting into the micro detail of what everything costs down to the last penny. They will do endless designs, endless tweaks. They'll say, 'OK, I need to talk to a manufacturer, but he's not available, he's on a business trip abroad, so I'd better wait until he gets back so that I can be absolutely sure I have the right figures.' And after those three months the numbers say it's not going to work. Any experienced entrepreneur could reach that decision in a day.

The whole principle here is to get to the point, for you to adopt the mentality of a Dragon, because we can make those decisions in twenty minutes. And you've got the luxury of seven whole days! The dynamic is that I am going to share with you my own thought processes, the kind of thinking I use on a daily basis. If you don't apply a similar process, it could take you a year to arrive at the same conclusion, but if you do you will reach your decision in seven days, tops – and more importantly your business will have a chance of succeeding.

Here is an example from very close to home. My wife Aisha happens to be a very talented, creative designer. She decided to create her own collection of clothes and I was happy to back her to start a business. We set things going and rented a shop space. Aisha spent a couple of weeks coming up with ideas, initial sketches and designs for her range, and then went to somebody who could make the patterns for those designs. To do that she needed to select and buy fabric which matched the designs, then have that sent over to the machinist. So she had a finished jacket, but that jacket had cost £200 to make, which meant we would need to sell it for at least £500.

Two things happened. I sat watching Aisha and I thought to myself, *She is putting in an awful lot of work to make that money.* In retail I need to spend £200 to make £500 because I've got the cost of the shop and the rates and the staff, plus I have got a speculative amount, and the cost of that capital and the opportunity of that capital. So already I was thinking that this was not a great business model.

Where so many people fail in their model is they do not include the cost of their time. So when I asked my wife to price up the garment she had priced the fabric, the cost of the machinist, everything other than her own time: she hadn't put anything in for the fact it took her three weeks to come up with the collection.

We put the range into the shop and we sold . . . not many, to be frank, because the price point for the jacket was very high. A few months later we went to see a wholesaler who was based in Paris. As he was showing us the ranges he had in his showroom, I noticed that one of his designs was quite similar to one of Aisha's, and, importantly, that I could buy that jacket direct from him for only £85. Now the jacket had been produced in a different fabric, and had a different concept, but in principle it would have done the job if you were going out for the evening, needed a smart jacket, but didn't want to spend £500.

I wasn't involved in the negotiations – Aisha was handling that – so I was just observing. My thought process went like this: *For £85 I could buy that jacket from the wholesaler. I haven't had to design it, haven't had to source the fabric, haven't had to make the pattern or hire the machinist. I've saved myself a month of effort. The cost to me is £85, which means I can sell the jacket at retail for £250, so (a) I've made more money and (b) I'm going to sell more items, because I'm retailing at half the price, and my opportunity versus cost of time is significantly better.* **Understanding the whole pricing journey is always critical.**

When we got back to London I sat down with Aisha and said, 'Look, why don't we just buy the range direct from the wholesaler?' She said, 'No, no, I don't want to do that.' 'Why?' 'Because I'm the designer. It's my boutique, it needs my brand.' I told her, 'I buy all of that. I understand why you feel that way. But let's look at this from another angle. Your time is currently uncosted and the cost per garment is double. Logically that tells me that we aren't ever going to make very much money. How many are we going to sell at £500 when that wholesaler in Paris has already produced ten thousand of those jackets? The principle of volume means you will never be able to compete.'

So she and I had a big debate. My view was, 'I'm not saying you *shouldn't* do it, but I think it's very important you understand what the consequences of your decisions are – because if you continue being a designer with your own brand, you won't be able to compete at the other end of the scale with the high premium brands like Chanel or Gucci. Your brand is simply not strong enough. Those companies are able to sell fewer units, but that's because Gucci can sell one bag at £1,000.'

In the end Aisha and I agreed not to manufacture ourselves, but to buy existing designer merchandise and resell it – and do you know what? We made a lot of money.

The concept of starting a business is that it should be customer-led and market-led, and shaped by customer response. It should never be the business pre-empting everything and then having to undo it all. How many new entrepreneurs apply that logic? In my experience, very few.

Does anybody really care?

I remember one guy coming into the Dragons' Den to try and persuade us to invest in a motorized shaving brush he had developed. In the final analysis, did the problem he was trying to solve ever exist? When we go out to buy things – and if we are not indulging in some pure retail therapy by impulse buying – then our decision to make a purchase is more often than not driven by the need to answer a particular problem. I buy a new tie because I am about to give a presentation at a seminar. There is a need to begin with. Now in the motorized shaving brush example, I've either already got a shaving brush or I can use my hand to spread the shaving foam and achieve the same effect. So I simply don't get the problem with the brush. And even if it did exist, did anybody out there really care that he had solved the problem? That is a very important, fundamental message.

In terms of price, common sense tells me that given a standard shaving brush costs £3 (assuming you aren't committed to owning the finest badger brush), if you then stick an electric motor in to drive it, the brush is going to cost you at a minimum double the price.

Would I pay a 100 per cent premium to solve a problem that doesn't even exist? What do you think? So the probability is that the product is not going to work. If he had been following our rule book I would like to think he would never have even developed the idea.

Then there was the chap who invented a motor-powered rotary clothes drier for his wife to speed up the process of drying his shirts in the garden even when there wasn't any wind. Now I think that I understand his mindset. He recognized there was a problem. Why? Because he's saying that drying clothes on the line if it's static takes two hours. And by putting a motor in they will be dry in only half an hour. That's the principle.

But, again, a standard rotary line costs you £10. His version using a motor, he said, would cost £70, even with cheaper components. And in addition to that, you would need to put in a slab of concrete in the garden to support the drier, and you'd have to run out an additional electrical power cable to drive the device. Is the problem he identified really so important that it justifies 600 per cent more cost plus all of the logistical nightmare of installing the machine?

If you sat down with a piece of paper and wrote on one side 'Problem: Two hours to dry my shirt vs half an hour' and on the other side 'Solution: Increase the price by seven times and organize and pay someone to lay a slab of concrete and run in the power cable?' the answer would quite clearly be: 'No'. It's not a business, is it? Do you know how long he had been working on that idea? Ten years. He was obsessed by working out how to dry that shirt in less than two hours. But he never asked the right question.

He was focusing on all the wrong issues. All he had to do was ask a different question, and that would have saved him ten years' work. Not least if he had thought about what was already available, he might have realized that there was already an established product on the market that did precisely the same thing: it's called the tumble drier!

That is why I always put so much emphasis on knowing the right questions to ask.

Do your research – it's critical

To analyse your idea you have got to do your research. It's fundamental. It's a deal breaker, success or failure. Research is key. If you don't do it, you're about to lose a ton of money.

Let's go back to the idea of setting up a café. The best advice I can give you if you're thinking of doing that is to go to ten different cafés in ten different towns or cities: in ten different areas, ten different brands.

Buy yourself a paper, go to the café, order up a coffee, sit down and observe. Observe *everything*.

Some cafés have great ambience, some are pretty sterile, some are quite fashionable, some serve great home-made food. When it comes to research, the key questions you should be asking yourself are: 'Why do they sell those product lines? Why do people come in? How long do people stay?'

The most critical element in the success of a café is footfall – the counting of actual or potential customers in a particular space. Footfall is the do or die of that business because it is a low ticket-value business. When you are in a business where the average sale is £3, you need a lot of sales just to pay the rent.

So the first question in my mind would be, 'What is the footfall?' Retailers employ research companies to send people to high streets, where they'll stand outside an empty shop with a clicker and at peak times count how many peoplewalk past the shop. Because if you don't have the right flow of traffic walking past that shop, you could have the best product in the world, the cheapest product in the world, but if there are not enough people to buy it, it will never work.

Imagine why a coffee shop in a very quiet location would never work. If you are in a secondary location, in a side street off the main road, the key difference is that on the main road the footfall is a hundred people, while on a side street it's ten. And how many of those ten are you going to convert and persuade to visit your café? **The principle of research is not that it's useful to know. It is critical to know.**

You can apply the same principles whatever business idea you have. And with the power of the internet you can also find out exactly what price points apply for similar products, what the competition is offering, within a short space of time. Look at your competitors' websites. Google the sector. Read articles about the kind of business you are thinking about setting up. Search for interviews by leading figures in that sector. Use all the information that is easy to access in conjunction with your own hands-on research. There's no excuse for not understanding the market.

I talked before about having the necessary personality to run a café: that outgoing, people type of person. The characteristics of a café owner are not the same as those of an analyst. If I look at my two daughters, Jemma would be a perfect café owner: she's gregarious, has great people skills, looks the part, sounds the part, possesses all the qualities. If you met her and heard she was opening a café, you'd say straightaway, 'Ah yes, I get it.' My other daughter Hanah has a degree in economics, is very mathematical, very focused, extremely analytical. She is also a people person but it doesn't come to her quite as naturally as it does to her sister.

If Jemma decided she wanted to run a café, the smartest thing she could do is to ask her sister, 'Hanah, can you help me? I need to do some research and analyse the café market. What do you think I should do?' Hanah would get it immediately; she'd say, 'You need to know the footfall,' because that's just the way her brain works. It doesn't mean Hanah's better than Jemma. They're just different. You have to find and recognize that difference and make sure you keep telling yourself it is not a question of being good or bad. It is a question of being different, and different is OK.

Whenever I come up against a problem, and I am not sure how to set about solving it, **the first question I ask myself is not 'How am I going to do this?' but 'Who do I know who can do it?'** Nine out of ten times I will know somebody. And so will you. I have found time and time again

when I'm faced with a dilemma, that while person A is trying –
and usually failing – to solve a problem all by themselves,
person B is working out who can help them solve it. I am very
much a 'Who do I know who can help me?' person. I always
believe that there are people out there who have different skills
from me who will be able to solve my problem not only better
but more quickly than I ever could.

A valuable part of your research will be going to trade events
and networking evenings. Every industry, every business, every
segment has its own events. I think every entrepreneur should
go to as many events as they possibly can. Once you know what
they offer, you can be a little more selective.

In whatever sector you are in, there will be seminars,
conferences, networking breakfasts, exhibitions, trade fairs,
online forums.

You will soon work out which are the most valuable events
for you.

There are still a lot of entrepreneurs who are reluctant to
attend these events. 'I don't know anybody, I'm not comfortable.
What am I going to do when I get there?' In a way, that helps
define whether you are an entrepreneur. To be an entrepreneur
you have to be able to do all of those things. And if you are not
confident enough to do them I would go back to the question:
'Do you really think you are ready to be an entrepreneur?'
This may be the first real test of your pain threshold, and the
question deserves a frank and honest answer.

For many people, going to events or trade fairs is not the
most enjoyable activity, but if you think of the potential

upsides, and how effective networking can be, you can really appreciate the value it offers. The more people you speak to about your business opportunity, the stronger the business will be.

Recently I was attending a property conference. On the final night I was sitting talking to some of the other delegates so late on that it was heading towards dawn, and by chance the guy sitting next to me said, 'James, I understand you are involved in real estate. I've got a cracking building you might be interested in.' It turned out to be a building right opposite my office, which was available at a competitive price and needed a quick sale. If I had not been at that networking event – and I was so tired that I was just about ready to turn in for the night – that opportunity would never have surfaced.

The JC twist

I have always found that whenever I go to any event, whether it's a trade show, a seminar or a talk, I always come back wondering why I don't attend more of them. Because I'll always meet somebody who tells me a snippet of information I didn't know, or suggests a different way of looking at a problem. The key thing is that these are called 'networking' events, so when you are there, please do network. Go and talk to people, approach people, introduce yourself and have a conversation. This is not the time or place to be a shrinking violet. Otherwise you'll end up wasting the opportunities on offer.

Getting on the train

Procrastination for whatever reason – because you can't see a way to resolve a problem, or because you are putting off the evil day when you have to confront the reality of your costing – is an absolute killer. I think of setting up a business as like taking a train journey. Far too many entrepreneurs end up sitting on the platform, wondering. They are the people who are never going to get anywhere. You have to get on the train to start the journey.

I will always get on the train. I come up with an idea and I can't wait to start the journey. But – and this is vital – I have already worked out whether or not it is worth buying a ticket for that particular train.

Let's say you start off thinking you want to open your own restaurant because in your neighbourhood there's not a great Italian place to eat. That's how it all usually starts. You've discovered the problem, there's no Italian near you. So why don't you look into opening your own Italian restaurant?

All of a sudden you have a couple of specifics. You are restricted to the area, because that's the problem you have identified – there's no Italian restaurant locally – and you've got a product, Italian food. As you go along the journey somebody is going to say to you, 'How much are you prepared to spend to set up the business?' 'Oh, I hadn't thought of that. I've only got £80,000.' 'Well, £80,000 isn't enough to open a decent restaurant.' That's annoying, but you turn the question round:

'What can I achieve with that £80,000? What *could* I open?' and now you're looking at a pasta place, because it doesn't require huge kitchens and facilities. The concept is still a variation on an Italian restaurant, just with cheaper product, cheaper stock, a cheaper fit-out, but you would never originally have thought of that solution.

The guy sitting on the platform, scared to get on the train, is still fretting about the intricacies and costs of a trendy Italian restaurant and meanwhile you have now opened a pasta place which has become one of the most successful pasta joints in the country, and before you know it you've opened a hundred shops. That's what happens in life when people succeed. They get on the train.

The converse to that is the guy who spends a fortune constructing a railway, dynamiting tunnels through mountains, building tracks to reach a particular destination. He's decided there isn't a way to get from A to B, and therefore, my God, there *must* be an opportunity. The question he failed to ask was whether anyone in A actually wanted to go to B. Had he asked that question, it would have killed the idea stone dead.

But he's so obsessed with blasting his tunnels that he's forgotten the most fundamental question. The railway tracks have been laid, the tunnels have been built, millions of pounds have been spent, the station opens . . . and there are no passengers. That's why we go back to research. That is why research is so fundamental.

In the same way that the customer and the market are what determines whether an idea will work, the truth of the matter is also that if you don't ever get off the ground, you are never going to have a business with a shape that can be determined. And once the journey is underway, that in itself will start to influence the path forward.

I like to cite the example of Richard Harpin, who founded Homeserve. He used to work as a management consultant at Deloitte and decided to be an entrepreneur. Realizing that finding a reliable plumber for an emergency was usually a nightmare, he set up a business to supply emergency plumbing on a 24/7 basis. With a £100,000 investment in place he started off only to find that his business model was not working: having hired in the plumbers he needed for all-day coverage, he found that many days he had some expensive plumbers sitting around doing nothing, and nobody needing any repairs. In the first year, the business lost £500,000, and he was going to have to find even more investment.

Rather than ploughing blindly on, he decided to recognize the problem and modify the business to sell cover for 'home maintenance services': in other words, if a household pays Homeserve £50 a month the company guarantees it will supply somebody – still with a rapid response – to fix a range of problems and emergencies in the house, anything from plumbing to electrics, a broken lock or getting rid of some mice. Suddenly his business model was radically different.

Richard Harpin had gone from hiring plumbers to running an underwriting business. Homeserve has over 3 million customers in the UK and another 2.4 million worldwide, and in March 2011 the company posted £116.6 million profit, with a valuation of £1.3 billion. It's a classic example of what can happen if you are strong enough to recognize that your first idea is not necessarily your best, and that the journey defines itself.

When I set up Hamilton Bradshaw I had no expectation that this company would become one of the country's leading private equity firms. It was never the plan.

The plan was that I had sold a business, I had realized some capital, and I wanted to invest the capital in a number of other businesses. My plan was there would be just me, a PA and an accountant. I would go out and find some deals, make an investment or two, my PA would run my diary, my accountant would make sure the numbers worked. I didn't really want to build another business.

My whole objective was to find a work/life balance. And do you know what? I failed! How did I get that so wrong? It proves that, like anyone, I'm not perfect. My boutique idea turned into a huge company. I'm back to where I started, I'm back to working hard seven days a week. Circumstances define success. For example, in my case, it was another event, namely joining *Dragons' Den*, that completely changed the course of my career.

Just imagine if you had opened your café, and six months after you opened up, a major company moved its head office into the building opposite. Overnight, you have 5,000 customers literally on your doorstep. You could never have planned that. Your business is going to rocket tenfold and all of a sudden you are thinking, *Maybe we should open three more of these cafés.*

In other words, don't worry about or plan your second café, your second outlet or your next product now because it's not relevant. When the first one succeeds, then it will all come to you. What happens in the future is a stage you shouldn't be wasting your energy on because if it's meant to be, you will get there.

The JC twist

I've recently been asked whether it is a good idea to try to set up a business in a period of recession. But when you think about success, is there ever a perfect time to bring out a blockbuster book, release an Oscar-winning film, or start a rock band? I really don't think it matters. What is important is not the timing, it is about you, your circumstances, your situation, your opportunity. I could give you hundreds of examples of people who launched businesses at what might theoretically have been the best possible time, economically speaking, but if their situation was wrong, and if their pain threshold was not high enough, they didn't make it. It's also very easy to blame the failure of a business idea on 'the recession' when the truth is it was never going to work in the first place.

The state of the economy is a factor, but it's not essential. The market economy is not the barometer – you are. The market is merely a guide. There are as many new businesses that succeed in a recession as fail in a boom.

Applying the process

When I came up with the idea of setting up a recruitment agency in 1985, I felt that I had stumbled across an unfilled niche in the market. In recruitment in the mid-1980s you had the headhunters at the top of the pile, very elite. Then came the middle-management agencies, whose recruitment was carried out through advertising in newspapers, and at the bottom was what I call the high-street market: big volume, with people walking into recruitment agencies off the street. I started doodling on a piece of paper and found I had drawn a pyramid with the headhunters at the top, the high-street recruitment companies at the base and the middle-management sector in between.

I sat there, studied my drawing and thought to myself, *Why is it that headhunting only exists up here at the top end, which is a small market in terms of numbers of people?* In the bigger middle-management band, where a salary might be £75,000 a year at today's rates, there were many more jobs – but nobody was headhunting in that space.

The interesting thing is that nobody had ever asked the question before. And when I asked why nobody headhunted middle managers, no one could give me a better reason than, 'Because we don't.' My light-bulb moment was when I realized that if an employer paid £10,000 for an ad in the broadsheets and it didn't work because Mr Perfect didn't happen to pick up the paper that Thursday, that was £10,000 wasted.

Headhunters receive one third of the first year's salary as a fee. If I were to start headhunting in this middle-management sector, the fee for a £75,000 salary would be £25,000, split one-third retainer, one-third shortlist, one-third completion. So the client would be committing to paying me £8,000 with no guarantee of me finding somebody who fits the job, compared to paying £10,000 for an ad, also with no guarantee.

I realized that there wouldn't be enough differential in the client's mind between my proposal and the existing way of operating. Their reaction would more than likely be, 'Thanks for the offer, James, but I'm actually OK the way things are.'

Then I thought, *Why do I have to charge a retainer? If I am going to headhunt the guy anyway then I don't have a cost.* That was my big driver: I realized the market had a fixed cost of £10,000. I had a zero.

So my twist was to say, 'I'll headhunt without a retainer. I'll guarantee you that I will find the right guy for your job. If I don't, you don't pay me. But if I do, I want £25,000.' Now I had a compelling proposition. I thought I could go out there and sell that proposition. I was sure I could convince a client with the pitch, 'I can find you the perfect person without you taking a risk. I will take all the risk myself.' It was a no-brainer.

The market was fertile because there was no competition. For every person I was going to call in the middle-management area, it would be the first time they had taken a call from a headhunter. In the senior exec positions, they had all been spoken to loads of times, all been pitched. But the middle-management area was virgin territory. So as the idea built, I got more motivated, because it kept ticking the boxes.

I had gone through all the steps I want you to do with your idea – I had identified the market, I had priced the market. Did my price work? Yes it did. I had crystallized my idea. Only then did I allow myself to start getting excited, not before. And I felt really excited because this was a huge market and nobody had ever pitched the idea at that level before.

Then I shared my idea. I talked to people I had worked with, people I knew in that sector, friends. One of them asked me a simple question: 'What are you going to specialize in?' And I hadn't thought of that. I didn't have an answer to the question. I quickly realized that if I was a generalist my credibility with the candidates would be very poor in those sectors I knew nothing about. It's hard to fake it.

So I eventually went into the field that I knew best, which was financial services. If I was going to have to pick one, why didn't I pick one I actually knew, so that I would be talking with credibility? Thank God I did specialize, because otherwise I might have failed.

Embracing the idea

And then I named the business, to make it mine. I looked at what the other headhunting businesses were called. At the time the main companies included Korn/Ferry, Russell Reynolds, Spencer Stuart and Heidrick & Struggles. All these people existed: there was a real Russell Reynolds, for example. I thought, *OK, there's a tip here. They are normally called after people.* But I didn't like the idea of calling it after me because, to me, that would sound like a one-man band. 'Hi, it's James Caan from James Caan Associates.' Somebody taking that call would just know they were being phoned by one guy operating on his own out of a tiny office.

The name, I thought, should say 'Big', 'Established'. As I said those words out loud, I wrote them down on my pad. I added 'Professional', 'Integrity', 'Dynamic'. I was describing what the business did. I wrote down a whole list of words, and then I thought if that was a person, what would it be called? I looked at my notes and, don't ask me why, but the name Alexander came into my mind. It felt right, because Alexander seemed established, professional.

I carried on musing . . . 'That's quite a long first name, it needs a fairly small surname, otherwise it's too much of a mouthful on the phone.' Very practical thoughts. But I couldn't come up with the surname. I got stuck. I tried a different tack: who is this business going to place in jobs, what kind of people are we going to be dealing with? They are all bankers, economists, senior executives. I wrote down the job titles and they were (and remember this was in the 1980s) all men. I wrote down Man, and added an extra 'n'! Alexander Mann. That was a name that suggested substance, integrity, gravitas.

Now I did that right at the beginning of the process. You need an identity for your idea. I think it's really important because it helps you focus. Once you've got the name for your business, whether it's a service or a product, it comes to life. **Whatever business you're going to be in, it's important to have that sense of identity, otherwise it's just air, it's just a thought.** But with a name, it has some substance. You can build on the idea.

To come up with the name Alexander Mann must have taken me less than half an hour of concentrated thought. I didn't employ a branding agency, I didn't bring in a designer to run through a hundred different concepts for a new logo. And today I wouldn't spend any time briefing a website designer. But I would have a name. It's part of crystallizing your idea.

Crystallization is the moment when your idea starts ticking the boxes, answering all the basic questions. The question today is: Does your idea work? Avoid getting caught up in all the micro detail, and focus on the key elements. Are you fulfilling a genuine customer need? If so, does the pricing make sense for that customer? Have you researched every aspect of the market in depth so you understand what makes it tick? And are you ready to embrace your idea, name it, and see where the journey will take you?

If the answer is no, be prepared to tell yourself, 'This is not going to work. I need to go back and start again. And I need to learn from what I've discovered about that first idea, and about myself.'

But if the answer's a yes, now you can get on the train. Welcome aboard. Oh, and don't forget to buy a ticket.

'There is no reason why, whether you are selling a product or a service, you shouldn't go out straightaway and get an order. Right from the off.'

DAY 3:
HAVE I GOT AN ORDER?

Once your product has stood up to the initial testing and you have a positive answer to the question 'Will my idea work?' you are in a strong position to move onwards: on to another day, on through another critical stage.

Getting aboard the train, as I like to think of it, is an active decision – choosing to act decisively – and this third day for your business idea is once again about moving on from imagining what could be to getting out there and doing something, taking actions that will really determine whether your business is ultimately bankable.

While I was thinking about what the next crucial stage in the process should be, I had my own epiphany. I realized the answer was quite straightforward. The answer is: getting an order.

If nobody wants to buy your product or your service, then you will have a very clear indication that you should put this particular idea to one side. To me that's still success, because nothing ventured, nothing gained.

Anyone who sets up a business follows the same process. We come up with an idea, we talk to a lot of people, we think about it. If the business is based around a product, most entrepreneurs will start putting time into patenting, arranging for a prototype to be made, going to the manufacturer, discussing the ins and outs, spending a year before it comes to anything.

If the business offers a service, the same happens: months and months cogitating about the brand, the image, the website, where the business is going to be located. Everybody's the same. I witness it every day of the week. It is very, very tempting to allow yourself to be distracted, to delve into all the detail and lose sight of what should be the key issue: Have I got an order, or will somebody give me an order?

What is the one thing that you need to do to attract investment? What is the one thing you can do that will make all the difference? It's getting that order.

The best way to prove that you are ready to secure an investment is to have an order in place. Investment readiness is when you have compelling information from third-party references that confirms the viability of your business opportunity. And the very best third-party reference is an actual order from a paying customer or client.

The moment you have an order in your hands your chance of securing an investment leaps from 10 per cent to 90 per cent. Or to put it another way, 90 per cent of the people who pitch to me do not have an order in place, and none of those 90 per cent end up getting an investment from me.

A close friend of mine, Gerry, whom I've known for twenty years, came across this incredible embroidery machine which basically meant he could take any garment and give it a bespoke embroidery treatment. So if you had a jacket or a shirt you could come up with a particular graphic, logo or image and with the machine he could embroider it on your jacket. For example for me, because of my *Dragons' Den* appearances, he created the shadow of a dragon in black cotton on my dinner jacket. Because it is in black on black, it's not immediately obvious, but if you were sitting next to me at a dinner you would see it. I thought it was a really strong idea.

Gerry came to me, showed me an example of what the machine could do on a jacket, and asked me what I thought. I told him I thought that there was a potential market and that he should develop the business. He went off and invested in the machine – spending £25,000 on that one piece of kit – and started producing all these garments.

I saw him a few months later and asked him, 'So how's it all going, Gerry?' He said, 'I've produced eight jackets and these are all the different styles.' 'Fantastic. What you need to do now is go out and start pitching this to retailers and see if you can sell them.' 'Fine,' he said.

Two more months went by. I bumped into Gerry again. 'How's it going? Have you sold any jackets yet?' 'Well, actually no, James. I've thought about what you said, but I think what I really need is to create a bigger range because all of the jackets I have at the moment are pretty much the same. I think I need different fabrics, some leather . . .'

I stopped him there, and said, 'To be honest, Gerry, I don't think you *do* need to do that. Because the principle of the jacket and the embroidered image would be enough for me as a potential customer to decide whether or not I was going to place an order with you. I might subsequently come back and say, "I really like it but I think I'm going to need some in leather." But you should wait for the customer to tell you that. Don't pre-empt them, because otherwise you've got to invest your own time, your own money, your materials, without knowing whether the market will buy that product.' He wouldn't budge. 'No. I think you're wrong, I think I need more range.' I said, 'OK, it doesn't make any difference to me. Great.'

A few months later we meet again. It's *déjà vu*. 'How's it going, Gerry?' He says, 'Well, I've done all the different fabrics, but I don't only want to do menswear, I think I need a ladies' range.' He goes off and does that. I see him again. Now it's turning into *Groundhog Day* . . . 'How's it going?' 'Yes, I've got the ladies' range, that's all in place. But I think I need to have my own branded buttons. I don't want to sell anything until I've got my buttons just right and I can put them on every jacket. I've designed them up and sent the designs off to the manufacturers. I should be getting those back in a couple of weeks. I'm also going to have my own labels designed. And then I need to set up a website.'

Another few weeks further on it's the same routine. 'How's it going?' 'I've got the ladies' range, got the men's, got the website up and running, got all the buttons and the labels have been sorted, they're looking great.' 'So have you sold any jackets yet?' 'No, there's just one thing left.' 'What's that?' 'I'm doing a photo shoot ...'

Now the reality in Gerry's case is that if he came to me as the customer, I really wouldn't care about the design of his label. If I wanted his label in a jacket, I'd tell him. If there was a chance I might want special buttons, all I'd need to see was an image of four different buttons, and I could choose from a, b, c or d.

Gerry didn't need to spend all that time or all that money on the kind of details that the customer didn't care about. And given that he hadn't in fact sold any jackets yet, there was no need for him to create a website because he didn't yet have a consumer product. Once he had ten customers buying from him on a regular basis, fine, but not until then.

Instead he could have designed the embroidery on a computer and shown how it would work on the jackets by using Photoshop. He could have produced a fabulous glossy presentation folder and included a selection of fabric swatches inside. He could have done all that within one week, versus spending a whole year perfecting every detail, without even knowing if there was going to be an order. Let's say he's earning £50,000 a year, he's lost £50,000 in salary, plus he's invested up to another £50,000. And he still doesn't have an order.

If you're developing a product, the question in my mind is, **Does the physical product tip the balance? I'm not convinced it does.** Because I would happily buy an item off the visual. Just think about all those apartments in Spain and Portugal that have been sold off-plan. The property developer has found a piece of land, bought it, brought in an architect to create a blueprint, mocked up what the development might look like – anything from an artist's impression to a brochure to a full-on video with animation – and has sold the development off the back of that. It's a virtual sale. And when he's sold enough of the apartments, only then does he start the construction work.

In the same way, if you were credible, if you were professional, if you had all the relevant information together, and a visual of your new product, what's the worst thing that could happen? I could say, 'You know what, I'll place an order subject to it being everything you say.' That's OK.

Imagine if you then come back to me, saying, 'James, I'm looking for an investment. I've got an order for 2,000 units with British Airways, providing I can deliver within six weeks.' Imagine how different the conversation would be. It's a conversation about a real order, about actual sales. That will significantly alter the balance between whether you get an investment or not.

How many times on *Dragons' Den* would we question the entrepreneurs about the orders they said they already had in place by asking, 'Have you got a letter of intent?' It was easy to sift out the ones who were claiming that they had orders from major chains, but under cross-examination it turned out it was the receptionist who had said in passing they thought the product looked nice . . . We spent time asking those questions for a very good reason: because it matters.

Yes, when you first go out and try to get an order, you may find that nobody is interested. As I've said, at least you have found that out good and early, and so from my point of view you have won. And, of course, if they say 'Yes', fantastic. It's game on. You are suddenly much closer to making your idea a reality.

Yet the knee-jerk response is always to avoid having your beautiful dreams dashed. 'I'm not going to talk to the customer. I need an office, I've got to put the website together, I need to hire people.' That's why those people might never get to the point of actually starting a business. They think all of those components are critical to their success but in reality they are a 'nice to have'.

It goes back to that point about paranoia. It's the guy who tells me, 'I can't really talk to a buyer yet because I haven't got my product patented,' when he doesn't even know if anybody's going to buy it. The fundamental flaw in that way of thinking is that you have to realize a buyer's job is to *buy*. Buyers are employed to look at products and decide which ones to purchase for their company. They are not inventors, they are not manufacturers, they are not interested in just one single product. If I'm the buyer at Argos I am busy buying 10,000 different items. I am not going to take time out of my busy life to copy your idea.

Thinking outside the box

One of the pitches to the Dragons was for a lockable box where delivery services like Ocado or Tesco Direct could leave orders safely if there was nobody at home. The creator had already spent nearly £1 million – yes, *one million pounds* – on that box.

If I had had that same idea I would have generated not only

a three-dimensional image, but one with animation, which has so much more impact. With the technology that is easily to hand, it's possible to produce graphics on your PC that are virtually (and that's the perfect word) as good as the product itself, without physically having to make it. After all, this idea is a lockable, refrigerated box, so understanding the overall concept is the key. The critical factor is not the niceties of the design styling; it's not the colour of the box.

Then I'd work out what the core market is: the supermarket delivery companies. So I'd start with somebody like Ocado, and go and talk to them. I've got my high-quality images to show them. 'Look, I've got this box, here's the image. This is what it looks like.' Then I'm into the pitch. 'We think it solves this problem: you can deliver when people aren't at home, so it widens your market.'

If they are interested they'll say, 'That's fantastic. I like it. Because if we could have a box like this, it would mean that rather than going backwards and forwards on deliveries, trying to liaise with the customers, changing times, getting complaints if we're not on time or they're out when we turn up, we'd be able to guarantee delivering on time. We could get that box and sell it to our customers and they'd put it outside their house. Sounds good . . .' The buyer, the potential customer, is just about ready to get on the train with us.

Then they naturally move on to the killer question: How much will it cost?

'It's going to cost you £50.' 'Well, at £50, James, we're not interested.' Right there, I've just saved myself £1 million of

R&D. Or the buyer's going to say, 'I'll tell you what. At £50 it's not going to work but at £35 I *would* buy it.' Brilliant. Because now I've got to go away and determine whether I can deliver the product at £35, because that's the price point that needs to work.

But, and you'll have to trust me on this, how many people do you think would do that? Hardly anyone. The crazy thing is, nearly everybody completes the product or service before they start selling it.

The reality is that until you start selling you will not get any customer feedback, and you will not know whether you have something people want to buy. Sometimes what makes the difference, what persuades somebody to buy, is one small element that might not have been obvious in the conceptual and planning phase.

The Addison Lee company is a great example of that. I first came across them a few years ago when I was out with the father of one of my daughters' friends and we had to order a cab. 'You must book Addison Lee,' he said. 'Why's that?' 'Because whenever you book a cab with them, they automatically send you a text to say the driver is on his way, his name is Bob Smith, this is his registration number and the price is going to be this.' He went on, 'I always feel really comfortable because if I am arranging a cab for my daughter, knowing the driver's name, the car registration, all of that, gives me peace of mind.' And since I was a parent with two daughters, I thought, *Yes, you're absolutely right*. A few days later I needed to organize a cab for my daughter Jemma to go out, and who did I use?

Addison Lee. Sure enough, in came the text with the details, and Jemma said, 'That's great, Dad, isn't it?' And it was still competitively priced.

With that one idea, which didn't cost the company much, a few pence per text at most, and which the car controller could slave off the computer booking system and the GPS in each car – a couple of mouse clicks and it's all there – the company had the compelling selling point that made all the difference. Now the company, founded by John Griffin with a single car, has 2,500 cars, all branded, smart vehicles, and is turning over £180 million a year. I love those examples of entrepreneurship where the critical factor is so beautifully simple.

Securing the order

One product I have invested in is the Motormouse. It's a fun executive toy, a cordless mouse which is in the shape of a sports car. Imagine you had come up with that. How are you going to break into a market which is already developed? There are loads of mouses out there.

For any product, functionality is key. What does it do? How does the Motormouse stack up against a standard mouse? It is cordless, it's aesthetically pleasing, the left and right clicks are on the front wings of the car, the headlights go on when you start using it.

Number one, there isn't a sports car mouse. At that level it is unique, for want of a better word. It will appeal to a certain group of people – largely men working in offices. It's a boy's toy.

So the object has functionality. It is aesthetically pleasing. The next element is the packaging, very important. Choose the wrong box and you could kill the idea stone dead. What's the most valuable thing in a shop? Shelf space. Put the Motormouse in too large a box and you're going to use up too much shelf space for the value of the product. How much is it going to cost? Let's say you're thinking £30, then it can't take up too much space. So straightaway there are more questions flashing up: Do I use a blister pack or shrinkwrap? How can I keep the space it uses to a minimum but still make sure it looks elegant, expensive, premium? All these things will affect the final price.

By now you'll realize without me having to tell you that most people who had that idea would spend ages on the design, go to a product designer, a graphics house, draw up a technical spec and make a prototype which would cost them a lot of money, maybe £25,000, and six months of time.

Do you know what I would do? I would pop along to my local Toys R Us. I'd buy a die-cast model of a Porsche or a Ferrari, any sports car. The point is I don't need to make it. And then I'd go to somebody buying product for a gadget store and show them the model. 'This is what we're thinking of. The mouse will work like this, and I am going to put a couple of buttons here.' The buyer would get the concept straightaway without worrying that this was not a working prototype. You can't even tell whether the bonnet has a right click or a left click. It doesn't matter.

'What price point are you thinking of bringing this out for, James?' 'I was thinking of £29.95.' The buyer, a genuine buyer, will tell me exactly what he or she thinks. They'll tell me if it's wrong for the market, if it's too expensive, too big, too small, too heavy. And I haven't spent any significant amounts of money.

When I invested in Motormouse, the team behind it had spent at least a year on their product. And remember at the end of the year nobody had bought it. Which is precisely why they decided to appear on *Dragons' Den*.

Look at the difference between that situation and me going in with my Toys R Us model car. Everything the buyer says is going to help me. 'I would be interested, but I think it's too heavy.' 'OK, how much lighter do you think it should be?' 'Well, probably 20 per cent – and by the way, I don't really like it in silver.' 'Oh, what colour do you think it should be?' 'I think it should be black.' All of a sudden I'm getting the best possible feedback, front-line research from somebody who knows exactly what they're talking about.

If the conversation continues along the same path, I'm going to walk out of that office with an order. And with the prospect of that order, the fundamental difference is that I then don't mind investing my time and money because I know I am going to sell my product. What I am not happy to do is waste a year of my life and risk at least £50,000, and that's not even costing in my time, which doesn't come for free.

If the buyer has said, 'Deliver what you say you can at the right price and we'll take a thousand of those as a first order,' then I'm in. Now I'm really motivated to build the prototype, but also I am building a prototype that fits the actual market, not what I *think* the market might be.

The JC twist

Feedback is precisely why you go and talk to the buyer. You will always learn something valuable. I would say that has happened on almost every idea I have ever had. One person alone can't know everything. And other people see things differently, they *think* differently from you. They might throw something into the discussion that could kill the idea. Or they will give you the one vital piece of information that makes the difference between you succeeding or failing. They might focus on something you hadn't even considered. That message is so important: you must not think that the buyer is being negative, that they are putting you off. My view is that, if they do tell you they are not going to buy, they are actually doing you a huge favour.

If I'd already designed the prototype, I'd have to go back and change that to fit the feedback from the buyer: make it lighter, alter the material, rethink the structure. That would be too much of a risk.

Instead, when I get back home after my meeting I can go back to Toys R Us, look at the model cars, choose the most suitable and find out who makes them. Google will provide a contact number and a name, so I can go straight to the manufacturer, explain what I want to do and ask them if they could make a modified version – put a groove here, add an element there – rather than having to find somebody to produce the mouse from scratch. A moulding costs a lot of money. The toy car manufacturer has already got the moulding. They've already put all the investment in.

Getting in to see the buyer

I'm often asked the best way to find and then get in to see the buyer who is going to place an order. The answer is: you Google them. You research who the end stockist is, and I guarantee you that somebody from the company will have attended a trade fair or an exhibition, or they'll be listed on the website.

Even simpler, just ring up the company and speak to the receptionist, tell them you need to write to the head buyer, so could they give you their name. And the receptionist will tell you. I used to do it all the time when we were headhunting. I would just ring the company and ask. If you were to ring Hamilton Bradshaw, and say, 'Hi, I have got a business idea and I'd like to write to one of your investment managers. Could you tell me who I should write to?' what do you think they are going to say? 'Peter Bright, Angela Smith'; the receptionist is always going to give you a name. It really is that simple.

Once you have your name, you contact them. If it was me, I would always phone first. If I can have a conversation with somebody, I find it much, much easier to start a dialogue than using e-mail. Let's say I've phoned my potential client's reception. 'I'm writing to your head buyer. Could you let me know who that would be?' 'Steven Leverage.' Great. I put the phone down.

I call back in and say, 'Oh hello, could I speak to Steven, Steven Leverage, please?' They'll put me straight through. If he's there, I don't hesitate. 'Steven, hi, it's James Caan here. The purpose of my call is that, very simply, I'm launching a new, unique concept for the executive toy market, which is a mouse for the computer in the shape of a Porsche. I strongly believe that if you go into most men's offices, they'd love to have something that they can identify with. **I just wanted to pop in and take two minutes of your time, to show you the idea. When would be a good time?'**

If Steven is in a meeting, and I get his voicemail, I'll leave exactly the same message, get right to the point. No messing around. I don't say, 'Sorry, I can't tell you what it is I want to show you until you have signed a non-disclosure agreement, but I'm sure you're going to love it.' Forget it. Because he won't be phoning you back. And of course I'll call all the other key buyers in the companies that might take the product. Every one of them.

Once an appointment is booked, I go on the net and I do a lot of research in preparation. Who's out there selling mouses? What's available now? What do they look like? How much are they? And the other important research I am going to do is, what does Steven Leverage sell at the moment? Because the fact I've gone to him means he must be selling something similar. Now if he's not selling some kind of souped-up mouse, that's great, but he's definitely going to be selling executive toys. I need the information as ammunition, because he's bound to ask me questions and I want to have sensible, informed answers ready.

However, when I get into his office there is one question I am going to ask him before he even gets the chance to test my knowledge of the executive toy market. Because who is the best person to tell me what this mouse in the shape of a Porsche is going to sell for? Yes, Steven Leverage. If anyone knows, he knows. He certainly knows better than I do.

So before he asks *me* the question, I'll get in there and ask *him* the question, 'So, Steven, this is the concept. Now, what price point do you think that should be?' And I guarantee you he will tell me what the range is. He will say something like, 'We won't get more than £30; £35 will be too much.' He will tell me upfront, because he knows who his market is, he knows who his customers are, he buys for a living.

Learning what the retail price will be is extremely helpful for an entrepreneur because 90 per cent of retailers use their own calculation for their mark-up. They have a strict formula and they stick to it. The calculation varies according to the particular sector, but in their minds they know that they need to mark up the unit price by a specific multiple – two and a half times, or double, or one and a half times, for example –

The JC twist

Now that the online market is growing so fast, you will be selling to buyers for online companies too. Online is all about price, because it is so easy to compare. When you're buying a TV online, what do you do? You use a price comparison website. Because generally you're buying a brand. A Sony 42-inch TV is a Sony 42-inch TV. You've got the spec. You've got the model. In that context, when you are selling to the online market you've got to understand that the critical factors are price, then delivery, and then availability. But always price first. The one big factor you'll have to overcome is that it is very hard to sell unbranded items that people haven't heard of online.

and that multiple will be the same for every buyer in the sector. How do you discover what that multiple is? Simple – ask the buyer. So, let's say Steven tells you that in the executive toy area, the retailer has to achieve at least a 100 per cent mark-up. That means you are going to have to sell the product to him for £15, and **that in turn triggers the question, What margin do you want to make?**

You've said to yourself that you've got to make at least a 20 per cent margin on any sales. So if you are going to get £15 a unit from Steven Leverage's company, you want to make a margin of £3, which in turn means you can't spend more than £12 making this mouse. Then you ask yourself where you are going to have the mouse manufactured. China. So you have to allow, say, £1.50 for shipping. Which means you've got to make it for £10.50. Then you've got to package it. The packaging is going to cost you £1, leaving £9.50. Then you've got the battery: 50p. You're already down to a manufacturing price of £9.

So when you go to your manufacturer you don't need to enter into a lengthy discussion. Your brief is really simple. 'I need to make this item for £9. What can you make for me at that price?' He'll say, 'At that level, it's going to have to be lighter. And the wheels won't be able to turn.' Perfect, but now you're in a brilliant position. Because if he says, 'I'm sorry, the absolute cheapest I can make this for is £12,' you'll know straightaway you're dead in the water. Although you'll be disappointed, how much better to know that now before you go any further. To use our train journey analogy, this is the stop to get off at.

Selling your idea

When you meet the buyer, what you – as the creator of the idea, the inventor of the product – bring along is the passion, the focus. People buy people first, before they buy the product. If you come in to see me, I've got to buy you first. If I don't click with you, if I don't connect, I'm not interested. You very rarely buy things from people you don't trust, people you don't connect with, people you don't like. Even if you like the product, but you don't like the person trying to sell to you, you won't buy it.

I had five people come in to sell me plants for my offices the other day. I had never bought plants before, but I felt the building needed some greenery. So I asked one of the receptionists to call five companies and get them to come in, and when they came in to see me I just happened to notice they were all carrying the same brochure, all selling off the one catalogue which contained the same plants. Essentially, each of the five companies had the same product. So why did I pick one and not the other? It was down to the person.

Lynn came in to my office, and immediately she was creative, animated and detailed. 'I think you need something here,' she said. 'It's got to be very green, and rich, but not too thick because of the border.' Just listening to her, I thought she knew exactly what she was talking about. I asked her, 'What about putting something over there?' 'Oh no, I quite like the pictures you've got on the wall here, so you'd have to have a very short plant to fit underneath them, and to be blunt it would just look a bit silly.'

And do you know what clinched it for her? It was really clever. We were looking at one particular corner of the office and she said, 'Have you got a minute?' 'Sure.' She ran out to her car, brought back a silver vase, and said, 'I was just sitting here and I thought I have something that would be exactly right.' There and then she put the vase down in the space and asked me, 'What do you think?' I said, 'Do you know what I would do?' 'What?' 'Leave it. It looks fine.' She clinched it there and then. In sales, that's known as the 'puppy dog close' – it's like saying, 'Why don't I leave this adorable puppy with you and your family over the weekend . . . ?'

That didn't sell itself, did it? She sold it. Because I hadn't even thought of putting something there. But Lynn knew exactly what she was doing. I wasn't even planning to buy, my objective was to talk to five different people, to get a feel for what they sold. But she was that one step ahead of the game. None of the other company reps even came close.

This is where we go back to the beginning. **I don't believe you can start a business if you are not passionate about it.**

I don't think you can fake it. Let's say you come across somebody running a plant business and hear that they're turning over £500,000 a year. You say to yourself, 'That's a pretty good business. They buy these plants in from China, they're landed at £200,000 and sold for half a million. I think I'll go into that business.' The critical difference is that you're not a Lynn. You couldn't sit here and size my room, you wouldn't be able to convince me what should go under my pictures or work out that the silver vase should go there. Nor would I be able to do that.

You will sell because of your passion, combined with everything we have talked about in this chapter. Those are the qualities – passion blended with salesmanship, market awareness, asking the right questions in the right order – which are the core components of an entrepreneur.

A critical stopping-off point during any entrepreneurial

journey is to validate these questions: Can I get an order? Is there a market out there? Will somebody buy this? And if they will, can I make it for the price they need to buy it at? Again, if the answer is no, get off the train at that station.

That is what we are all trying to analyse, and often over-analyse. My view is, why not just go and talk to somebody, and ask them if they would buy your product or your service, because you are going to have to do that anyway at some point? Don't put it off to the end of the process, because however long you leave it, you are still going to have to go out and do exactly the same thing. Why not do it at the beginning?

Get your first order, and you are still in. You're still on the train.

'However exciting the feeling of landing your first order is, if you can't deliver it and make a profit, it's a false dawn. But don't cheat the costs just to keep the deal, and your dream, alive.'

DAY 4: DOES MY COSTING WORK?

By the end of our seven days I want you to find yourself in a position where you are able to evaluate whether the business idea you are working on is a genuinely bankable proposition. Ideally, at that point you could in theory – or in practice, why not? – walk into the *Dragons' Den* and find yourself an investment.

If you are still on the train on Day 4, it's because you have got yourself an order, or your first client. That is the launch pad for everything else that follows, because now you are dealing with two realities: tangible income and definable costs. You are also at the point where everything can very quickly evaporate, because you now have to work out whether your idea can turn a profit, and if so whether that profit is enough.

Every solution to a problem is attractive – at a price. If, for the sake of argument, I want to go from my house to my office in the West End I have to make a choice. I could take the tube for £2.50 or jump in a cab that, with a tip, might cost £15. On a purely financial basis going by taxi is not a great solution. It is *a* solution, and of course it gets me there quicker, and it is likely to be more comfortable, but financially it doesn't make sense.

In the same context, 90 per cent of the people who come up with great business ideas are at least six months in before they turn round and ask themselves, 'How much will it cost?' Rather than waiting until Day 184 to ask that question, we are going to ask it on Day 4.

Don't be fazed by the spreadsheets

You don't have to be a spreadsheet genius to work out the costs of your business. You can do your business forecasting on a piece of paper, without Excel. Because I will let you into a little secret. Doing the costing is a piece of cake. People love to make a big drama out of it, but how difficult is it really?

Let's say I am planning to set up a business selling insurance. I find a sheet of A4 and do a monthly breakdown. In January, I'm going to employ Bob, Steve, John and Suzie, and I'm going to pay them each £2,000 a month. So four people, that's £8,000 a month. My rent is going to be £1,000. My printing costs are £500, my phone bill is £100, my stationery £75, various other bits and pieces will come to £325, so my costs in January are £10,000. The income for that month is £12,000, so that leaves £2,000. **Doing a costing is that easy. Is it money coming in as revenue or money going out as costs?**

What I'm saying is that really anyone with a calculator can do that costing. It is the most basic process of adding up and taking away. Because I am the CEO of a private equity company, everybody assumes I am some kind of accounting whizz-kid. I am not. But I am very good at adding up and taking away. I just put down what comes in, take away what goes out, and what is left is the profit.

Valuing your time

One of the reasons I am always so keen to get into the nitty-gritty of any business quickly is because I value my time. Most first-time entrepreneurs have little sense, if any, of the cost to them of the time they are dedicating to developing their idea.

In all your costings and your projections you must build this in, otherwise you are merely creating a false and unsustainable projection. In the example above, I should also be adding in my own £2,000 salary, which immediately wipes out any profit.

Let's say you are earning a salary of £45,000 a year at the moment. You have decided to leave your job and start up a new business that requires an office. When you cost the business, you will automatically put a figure in for the rental costs of the office, but you must, just as automatically, add in the costs of your own time. Because if the business is not able to absorb your costs, it is never going to work. And even if you have decided you can afford in the short term not to pay yourself out of the business, maybe because you have just received a pay-off from your last full-time job, remember that your budgeting should be based on assumptions of cost, not actuals. At some point you will still need to take that salary out of the business.

If in your costing you put in a line for your £45,000 salary and the business is now making a loss, that tells you straightaway that the business model you have created is not a sustainable one. The business only works if it has true cost. Taking your income out artificially creates a profit, but the moment you come to the next year and say, 'By the way I want to take £45,000 a year out,' it crashes.

This always, always happens. Three-quarters of the entrepreneurs who turn up in *Dragons' Den* have forgotten to cost in their salary. They always say that they are not taking any money from the business, stressing it as if they believe it is a really positive aspect. Of course, at one level that is great because it demonstrates their commitment, but from a business point of view it costs money to deliver the service. And not putting it in is artificial. How long can they genuinely carry on working for nothing?

Treat yourself exactly as you would any other employee. When you sit down and draw up the costing you will say, 'Brian, John, Helen, these are the people, this is their salary and their National Insurance. That is the cost of employing them.' Now do the same for yourself. You might want to put in a little less than your current earnings – or maybe put in a little more! – but you have to recognize that what you are doing represents a cost to the business, **unless you want to do this for the rest of your life for free. Which clearly you don't.**

An additional problem is that not including the cost of your time distorts your selling price. Whenever you don't add your cost in, the selling price, whether it's for a product or a service, appears to be cheaper. Without your cost in, the price works, *but only on paper*. Now, if I have become one of your customers or clients, you try re-pitching to me once you have decided to take a salary out of the business and as a result your price has risen by 30 per cent. I will not be prepared to pay you the increased amount, because you started off with an artificially low price. The initial success of your business has been illusory.

In *Dragons' Den* one guy came in who had created a business which would rent out expensive items of jewellery. His idea was that there were many people out there who owned some amazing pieces of jewellery which spent a large amount of time sitting in a jewellery box or a safe and were only worn once or twice a year. The concept of his business was that rather than letting the jewellery sit about doing nothing, the owner could send an image of it to him and let him load it up onto his website. Then if somebody else was going along to a gala black-tie event, rather than buying something new or using costume jewellery, she could decide she'd love to wear a stunning original piece – and why not rent it for the night? He planned to rent out a tiara worth £10,000, for say, £400, which he'd split with the owner. He'd use a security firm to do all the couriering. In principle, not a bad idea.

Cut to the studio. All the Dragons are thinking that in this current economic climate the idea of hiring out jewellery might work. Alan, who is making the pitch, has spent ten years at a top-flight jewellery manufacturing company, he's in his late thirties, is smart, looks the part, has an immaculate background and has delivered a great pitch. We are now into the twenty minutes of Q&A and I can sense that we are all building up to making Alan an offer, because it all seems to stack up.

Deborah starts probing. 'Alan, we like you, we like the concept. Talk us through your projections.' He says, 'In the first year I think I'll make £50,000 profit, second year I'll make £75,000, third year £110,000, on very little cost base.' It sounds reasonable. The others are asking their questions and meanwhile I am looking at Alan, thinking he looks quite an impressive character, very polished, very professional, and I am reflecting on the fact that he's been ten years at a company dealing in diamonds and premium jewellery where he must be earning good money. So when I had a chance to question him I said, 'Could I ask you what your current salary is?' He paused, looked at me and said, 'It's £135,000.'

'Hang on a minute,' I said, 'that doesn't add up. Forgive me, Alan, but to me, when people start a business there are two fundamental principles that you take as a given. One is that as a business if you invest £1 you need to make £1. You very rarely look at a business where you invest £1 to make 50p, so on that basis I have a problem.

'You have just told us that in Year 3 you're going to make £110,000 and today you're on a salary of £135,000. What you haven't factored in is that if you do this business you are actually risking £135,000, because today that is a guaranteed salary. You get paid whether you perform or not. Why would you give up £135,000 to make £50,000, £75,000 or even £110,000?

'And I am also going to assume that anyone who comes in to me and pitches me a projection is always going to pitch me at the top end of their range. Nobody pitches at the bottom end of a range. So in Year 1 you will be earning at least £85,000 less than you were earning before, and in Year 3 you are still earning less.'

In response he came back with, 'In fact, I'm trying to be very conservative with my projections and I didn't want to over-egg them.' 'But the problem I've got, Alan,' I said, 'is that whether I think they are high or low in reality doesn't matter because I am not running the business. You're the person who has put in ten years with your company, you've done your numbers, you've carried out your research, you've made your projections, you've incorporated your assumptions and you believe the profit in Year 1 is £50,000. So I believe that it will do what you think it will do. **The problem is, if there's not enough money in it for you, how do I make any money out of it?**'

That one question killed the deal. If I had not asked him the question about his salary, I am sure we would have gone on to make him an offer, because up until that point everything was looking great.

Building in the sensitivities

As well as not costing in time, another element I frequently find is missing from a costing is the impact of seasonality: irregularities that occur at different times of the year. It is a huge factor.

Every business contains some degree of seasonality. For example, one of my businesses supplies teachers to schools. When I first looked at the business plan, since I didn't really know that sector I forgot about the fact that they effectively only trade for thirty-nine weeks a year, because a teacher spends only thirty-nine weeks in the classroom once the school holidays are stripped out. That means that if I am providing teachers, for thirteen weeks of the year I have no market. The problem for that particular business is how to cover its costs during those thirteen weeks.

What people generally say is, 'We are going to generate about £20,000 a month,' and they put down that £20,000 for each of the twelve months. For them it is a straightforward linear calculation, but to me it actually demonstrates a lack of awareness of business realities.

If you have a cash-flow business operating on a weekly basis, you have to remember that some months include five pay days. Understanding the implications of that is a major issue: for example, I pay temps every week. In a month where I have to pay them five times, what do you think my failure to allow for that would do? It would kill my profit.

There is also true seasonality: the fact that many people are away on holiday in the summer months has a direct impact on the revenue of many businesses. For most companies, summer is a period when revenue is going to drop. For other businesses, perhaps one that is dealing with coachloads of schoolkids coming to the UK from Europe on exchange visits, that is going to be their peak time. So whenever I look at a projection and

I see that seasonality has been built in, it tells me that this entrepreneur has been digging down beneath the surface figures.

There are less obvious forms of irregularity that might affect your company. For example most entrepreneurs proposing to start a business that employs sales staff will show me a business plan that starts the year with five or six salespeople and ends the year with the same five or six. But how many sales businesses do you come across which have 100 per cent retention of their sales staff? Very few. When you are relying on each salesperson contributing month in, month out to make your business plan work, again the linear line looks good, but it is not realistic.

If you are costing a business based on retailing a product, how often will you sell 100 per cent of what you produce? Why do retail businesses hold sales and special offers? To get rid of obsolete product. So you start off with 1,000 units retailing at £100, you sell 75 per cent of them at £100, another 20 per cent at £70 as a reduced price to clear the line, and you'll be left with 5 per cent of them that you can't shift. Time and again I see business proposals where the assumption has been made that every single one of those 1,000 units sells at full price.

The other classic mistake is forgetting about discount. You would think it's incredibly obvious that any discount should be included but you would be astonished how often it is left out. When somebody is desperately trying to convince themselves they have a great business venture, they subconsciously blinker themselves. If they put their product in at full price the business makes money, but if they put the discount in, it loses money.

What happens when Lara, who delivers £10,000 or so in sales a month for you, decides to leave your business? You start the year off, she's working for four months, but she bills next to nothing because she's already thinking about the next job. You've lost all that money, and you have to start again. You have a two-month gap here, because by the time she leaves, you'll give her a month's notice and it takes you another month to hire someone. Now you've got Months 1–4 with nothing in, but a negative liability, two months blank again, then the new employee starts, blank again for the first two months as he settles in, and then he finally gets up and running. Now you are into Month 9 before you can start entering the revenue from the new guy.

So where you might have projected that this particular sales position is going to contribute £100,000 in the year, the actual contribution is less than £40,000. Which doesn't look so great. What is that going to do to your plan? Hence why it is so important to prepare some sensitivities. If you are asking me to make an investment, and as I'm reading through your proposal you tell me that in your figures you've taken into consideration that you're going to turn over 20 per cent of your workforce, I'm already thinking to myself, *Good. Smart.*

So they ignore the discount, because they don't want to let go of the dream.

When you look at the average business, the net profit as a percentage of turnover is anywhere between 5 and 15 per cent. So if you haven't included discount, as soon as you give away a discount of 15 per cent you've effectively wiped out your entire profit. It drops straight to the bottom line, because you have to absorb all the cost whether you give discount or not.

In a service business, you also have to factor in staff holidays, or more accurately the human nature that comes into play around holiday time. Generally a staff member will take six weeks' holiday in three lots of two weeks. My experience has been that in the week before they go off on holiday, they're already unwinding, and not producing anything useful for the business. And when they come back, nicely tanned and relaxed, they need a week to answer the e-mails in their inbox, to catch up on the backlog and restart. Again it's hardly productive time. When you add that up over three holiday breaks it represents the best part of three months of unproductive time.

Guess how often I get to see a business plan where the forecast shows that at Easter Jim's not there, so revenue plummets, summer he's not there, it plummets again, and December ditto. Or a plan that assumes some of the staff will fall ill. Hardly ever. I am not saying you should assume that everybody is going to be sick, but if you have five people working for you, it is fair to say that during the course of the year one of them is not going to be feeling on top form for a week or two. Build in that element or you will be sitting back and admiring a linear graph that says you are going to generate *x* amount of money. And surprisingly enough you won't.

If you'd got it right in the first place, you might have looked at the plan very differently. You might have made some very different cost assumptions. However, all your assumptions are based on the fact that you think you are going to make this huge profit at the end, and maybe, just maybe, if you'd run the plan correctly in the first place, included all the sensitivities, taken the stock into consideration, recognized that for three months of the year your people are not fully productive, you might have taken a second look at the costs and said, 'It's not worth doing. There's just no money in it.'

Which goes back to my recurring theme: Is it a business?

Realizing it can work

When I was thinking about setting up Alexander Mann, my recruitment company, I realized very quickly that my business had a limitation because I personally could only generate a certain amount of income and therefore I was only as good as the weeks I was able to work.

At that point I decided that in order for me to turn this idea into a business I needed to replicate and scale out the work that I was doing. I needed to find people like me. At the time I was in a fortunate position because the recruitment industry had 100,000 other recruitment consultants who worked for other people. If I could hire somebody and pay them 40 per cent of what they billed I would take 60 per cent of their billings.

I happened to have an office which could hold three people, so I realized that if I hired two other people it wouldn't cost me any more overhead, because my office costs were already being covered. The only incremental cost would be in the phone bills, and the additional salary, but if the first person I hired was billing £10,000 a month, and from that I was able to take £6,000, with two people in place I would be taking £12,000, plus what I was already billing myself which was £15,000, so my £15,000, less overheads, was all profit, *plus* I would be making another £12,000 on top.

By Year 2 I was making £250,000 a year. Not surprisingly, I was feeling good. I wondered to myself whether I could increase the staff even more, so I took a larger office and hired four more recruiters. Over the following six months I hired two more, and now I was in a position where I found myself struggling to put in the time to continue billing myself as well as managing the eight staff I had brought in – and I was still the biggest biller in the office. At that point I was quite scared because I discovered I could not manage staff *and* carry on bringing in my own billings. I wasn't doing a great job of either managing the eight staff or looking after my own clients, and my business was starting to crumble round the edges.

I had to decide whether or not to take a gamble and drop out of generating revenue myself, which was quite frightening because that had always been my safety net. In my subconscious I had been able to tell myself, 'Well, if everything else fails at least you can get back out there and do it yourself.' I couldn't make up my mind so I took a two-week holiday in Italy. I was sitting on the beach and reflecting on this problem every day because it represented that big a decision for me. My conclusion was that if I didn't make a change, I already knew where I was: I had a boutique business and so I would always be a boutique because if I continued to bill there was a limit to what I could do.

I decided to gamble and stop billing, and to put all my focus on the eight people that I had in place. As a result I would be losing, for the sake of argument, the £15,000 a month I was currently billing. However, if by dropping out of actively selling I could improve the productivity of the existing staff sufficiently to replace, or more than replace, my existing £15,000, that was a decision worth taking.

The gamble paid off. The new business model worked exceptionally well. I was able to build up the staff to twenty recruiters. And I now started thinking to myself, *This feels like a real business. It's no longer a lifestyle business. So what I really need is two managers, one to run each team of ten.*

I worked out in my head that if I could hire two good managers, that would give me back 80 per cent of my time. Because although I would still have to manage those two managers, that would only take up 20 per cent of my time. In the 80 per cent spare time I now had, could I go out and recruit another team of eight? Yes. So I hired in two managers. I spent 20 per cent of my time managing them, and that freed me up to go off and recruit another team of eight. And I went from that model to a business which employed 116 revenue earners.

But I had not started out planning for or imagining a company with 116 revenue earners. I had started off with just me and then two other people and at each stage I had made sure that the basic costs worked. The later success of the company came from getting that right from the outset.

Passing the smell test

If you are in the business of buying property, as I have been, it is tempting to over-theorize and over-engineer. You are sent some details about a commercial building, which look interesting. You ask all the usual questions. Location? How much is it on sale for? What's the rental income? You've got to get a survey, you need to get lawyers. But before I get dragged into all that I want to know if it passes what I call 'the smell test'. I'm not talking about the quality of the drainage system, I'm talking about the deal.

Let's say the building is going to cost £10 million, the rental income is £100,000 a year, and the tenant is a start-up business. The bank is never going to lend me money with a start-up tenant in place. If I sit down with the bank and ask them to lend me 60 per cent of the value, £6 million, one of the first questions they will ask me is, 'Who's the tenant?' 'It's Joe Shmoe.' 'How long has he been in business?' 'Two years.' 'Forget it.'

It doesn't matter what the building is or where it is. It doesn't matter how good the lifts are, how cutting-edge the décor is,

Always retain some flexibility. Remember my Motormouse example. Our buyer wants to sell the mouse at £29.95 tops. There is nowhere to go up from there. If I go away following the first meeting, do all my costings, and then head back into his office and say, 'Steven, I can make the mouse, and I can deliver all the specifications we agreed, but it actually needs to retail for £49.95,' I'll have wasted my time, and his. He's going to show me straight to the door.

But if I go back and tell him, 'Steven, I'm in a position to deliver the Motormouse for you. It will take us three months to delivery and I can get it to you at the price you need,' I will be able to put an order in the book. The price he needs to buy at because of his internal formula for marking up is £15.00. My ideal cost price was £12.00, because I wanted to clear £3.00, a 20 per cent profit for me. But in fact despite a lot of wrangling with the manufacturers, the very best production cost I've managed to get to is £12.50. Now Steven doesn't need to know that. He's not interested in my profit, just his. To secure the deal I have taken a view. For now I am prepared to take a slightly reduced profit. I don't make 20 per cent, but I make 16 per cent. That I can live with. It doesn't destroy me. It's not perfect, but it gets me rolling. And once the orders start coming in I'll be in a stronger position to negotiate down the manufacturing price because of the quantities I'll be dealing in. And next time round I can hit my 20 per cent target.

the fact that it's just had a complete rewire. The bank is not going to lend you the money.

The inexperienced entrepreneur goes along to view the building and falls in love with it. He gets over-excited, phones all his mates to come and take a look. He raves over the fantastic location: it's got a secure car park, it's only five hundred yards from the tube station, the shops are just round the corner. He spreads out all the floor plans, calculates the square footage, starts dividing up the space. The air-conditioning is brand-new, the IT network is state of the art.

It's all irrelevant. Because he can't buy it.

In every business situation you have to apply the smell test. The problem is knowing what it is. I've been around long enough now that when somebody rings me up and gives me all the spiel about how this property is right next to Harrods, has been entirely refurbished, has beautiful panelled walls . . . if I can't get a mortgage on it, it doesn't matter.

The same applies when you buy a house. If you're not earning the salary that at three and a half times equates to the mortgage, it doesn't really matter how wonderful the house is. But you could be wasting at least six months finding your ideal house, because it's detached, got a large garden, a great room for the baby – only to find, hello, it's not in your price bracket.

I'm always looking for that critical element that means the costing won't work. Equally, I am looking for the gem, the one thing that gives me the green light.

Back to our commercial building, rewind to my chat with the bank. 'So, who's the tenant?' 'BT.' Ah, now the bank will lend me money on that proposition. They might even give me 70 per cent of the equity value rather than 60 per cent. Now I'm in. Now I'm really interested. Now I'm delighted to go back to the building, talk through the details of its air-conditioning system: what make was it, how long's the system been in? Is the building fully carpeted? When was the last refurb done?

I'm not going to waste all my time if it didn't pass step one. It is exactly the same in every business. Yet in all the pitch meetings I have, probably less than 10 per cent of the people I am talking to have identified what the 'smell test' in their particular business proposal is and the criticality of that point. To use the analogy of the property example, they haven't worked out the relevance of who the tenant is. They'll have spent three months, produced spreadsheets and research and due diligence, and gone to all the banks only to be told no.

To make you feel better, I still don't always get it right. When Hamilton Bradshaw started off we were working on one deal and over-analysing it to death. Six months down the line we decided we were not going to go ahead with it. We made the decision late on a Friday. And two of the guys who had been working on it for me left the office demotivated almost to the point of resignation.

All weekend this was really bugging me. I was turning it over and over in my mind. It was a really bad outcome because as a firm we had invested six months of our time, our costs, our research, our people. I calculated it had cost us in the region of £250,000 before we had walked away. On the one hand I was arguing with myself, saying, 'We did a great job, we were so thorough, it was absolutely the right decision,' and on the other I was asking myself, 'Why on earth did it take us so long to reach that conclusion?'

And the answer was really simple: we hadn't focused on the equivalent of who the tenant was. We had been so drawn into all the detail that we had forgotten to ask the right question. When I came back into the office on the Monday I looked at the deal again and thought, *Where is the tenant question in this?* And there it was staring out at me. I had found it, but it was too late.

Somebody said to me many years ago – and this has stuck in my head ever since – 'If you're going to fail, James, make sure you do it quickly.' At the time I didn't get it. It seemed like a ridiculous statement. But when you actually think about it, what a great line that is. **If you're going to fail, make sure it happens quickly.** Because then you can get it over and done with. What do most people do? They procrastinate failure. They drag it out.

Look at your costings. See if you are missing the obvious. Make sure you are not kidding yourself.

It all goes back to today's question: Does your costing work? Go through all the income assumptions, all the costings. Is there a profit in there? Have you added in the cost of your own time? Have you built in the sensitivities? And does it pass that critical 'smell test'?

Double-check the costings. Then double-check them again. And then get somebody else to check them. If the costings survive that level of analysis, you can feel confident of moving on to Day 5.

'Usually one person cannot be the ideas genius, the financial wizard and the salesman rolled into one. Genuinely multi-talented business people are few and far between.'

DAY 5:
HAVE I PUT TOGETHER THE RIGHT TEAM?

A common preconception of an entrepreneur is one person acting alone and not only coming up with a series of brilliant business ideas, but taking all the decisions, doing all the work, and consequently reaping all the rewards.

There is a grain of truth in there, but setting up your own business doesn't have to be such a solitary, lonely journey. That impression is probably fostered by entrepreneurs who are so paranoid about protecting their latest world-changing idea that they operate like hermits and refuse to confide in anybody else.

My philosophy is to turn that thinking inside out. Just as you should try to get as much feedback on your original idea as possible, because it is always going to come back stronger and tougher, so you should make the entrepreneurial journey with the help of other people. The burden on you will be lighter, and the decisions you take at critical forks in the road will be better.

It is very rare that a business proposition can be fulfilled by a single person. A one-man band is usually not a business. It's a hobby. That's Uncle Jeff in his shed making his stand-up shovels.

Coming up with the idea and then deciding to go off and start a business is too simplistic a sequence of events. You need to understand first and foremost who you are and what you are, what you personally bring to this new business. Are you a marketeer? Are you an inventor? Are you a financial expert? Are you a manufacturer? Whether the idea is a concept for a product or service, for a business to have some chance of success, you need to be able to have access to the full range of expertise that will allow you to fulfil the constituent parts the business requires.

In the human body, we have a heart, lungs, kidneys, a brain, eyes and ears. Each organ of the body plays a specific role and contributes to the body functioning healthily. A business is much the same. You need a heart with the passion of the entrepreneur, the brain to control the planning and financials, legs for distribution . . .

If you have nobody involved in your business who can help financially, who will manage and protect your accounts, forecast your cash flow, it's going to be a case of the blind leading the partially sighted. And you will inevitably make a mistake somewhere along the line.

As you look at the shape of your business idea, ask yourself who is going to handle the financials, because if you are the person who's come up with the original idea, you are quite probably not going to be the finance expert. You're the inventor.

It is unlikely, though not impossible, that you will have the skills to cover both bases. But if your idea does take off somebody will quickly need to look after the financial side, register the company, sign up for VAT, sort out PAYE, put together a cash-flow forecast, determine how much money you're going to need, how much money you're going to burn. Who is going to do that? If you don't have anybody in place yet, maybe you still haven't got a workable business idea.

The financial role is always going to be critical to your success. Most businesses that fail go wrong because people run out of money. And why do they run out of money? Because their financial planning doesn't project it. So, let me ask you again: Who is going to do that? If the answer is, 'I don't know', **that's akin to saying, 'I can design the car, but I have no engine,' or 'I've got the engine, but I've got no fuel.' It is not going to work.** You need to accept that if your business lacks that component of financial expertise and management, you might as well not bother.

The answer is to go and find somebody who can manage the finances. In the early stages you can outsource it – hire in a company who can provide you specifically with that service. Use an accountant. What's the worst that can happen? They will charge you for a few hours' work. It's not the end of the world. At this stage I'm not looking for micro, I'm looking for macro, looking at the big picture. In the first instance I would not go out and hire somebody, with all the implications that involves. I would look on the web, tap in 'accounting services' and find a company based locally that offers what I need – and no more;

there's no need to sign up with PricewaterhouseCoopers just yet.

Later on, as things start moving forward, then bring somebody on board to work with you. Maybe you can't pay them initially, so offer to make them a partner. Find somebody who has that particular strength in accounting and who also shares in your vision, someone who is prepared to say, 'OK, you've convinced me that this is a strong idea. I'll come in with you. Give me 20 per cent and I'll become your partner and look after your finances.' At least you've got 80 per cent of something that might work versus 100 per cent of something that otherwise is possibly never going to work. It's all relative. The only reason you are talking to them in the first place is that you lack the particular skill set or experience they possess. Which essentially means that if you go and do it yourself the chances are you're going to come up with nothing.

As well as bringing in somebody to oversee the finances, ask yourself who's going to sell your product or your service. You know that getting the initial order, securing the first client, is a vital stage in this journey. But again, maybe selling is not for you.

The odd thing is that almost every entrepreneur believes they are God's gift to sales. Because they are passionate about their own idea, they imagine that nobody else on the planet can fail to see how brilliant it is.

The truth is that the vast majority of people who pitch a business idea could not sell toffees to kids. Just because you came up with the idea doesn't mean that you can sell it. Sales, selling, pitching, negotiating, closing a deal, together these constitute a real skill, some would even say an art form. That whole subject alone is a book in its own right. The reason is that knocking on doors and facing rejection every day is not something that the average person has the ability to absorb. Most people in that situation will give up, and consequently will probably lose their money. In that context you must at least ask yourself the questions, **What's involved in the sales process? Who am I going to sell to? And who is going to sell the most effectively?**

This is another time to be honest with yourself about areas in which you have no natural ability. When you have to pitch to a buyer or a client then, unless you are a natural salesperson, take somebody along who does know how to sell, someone with the right knack, who has those critical people skills, who can communicate at the right level and present your idea in a way that the buyer will understand and appreciate very quickly.

But, you might say, 'I don't know anybody like that. None of my friends or family are in sales.' That might be true. But imagine if I said to you, 'Find me somebody you know who is good at presenting, and who you think could clinch a deal, but who might not necessarily be a sales manager or a sales director.' I bet you'd know somebody if you thought about it.

When I'm trying to hire somebody to sell on my behalf, my immediate thought is, *Who's sold me something like that before?* Let's say a company owes me money and I'm going to have to sue them. I need to find a lawyer. What's the first thing that comes into my mind? When was the last time somebody sued *me*?! Which lawyer did *they* use? It's the same principle as when you're trying to sell your house. When you're looking for an estate agent, invariably the first person you'll call is the one who sold you the house.

However, if I do draw a blank, my next question is, 'How can I locate that particular kind of person?' In the recruitment business, whenever I was taking down a client's requirements for an employee I'd ask, 'So, Brian, you're looking for a finance director. You know the profile, the sort of background they have, the qualifications they need. They've been working in financial services and earning this kind of package.' Then I would follow up with the killer question. 'OK, you've described in detail the person you want. So where are they now? Where are they working?' And incredibly, the client would tell me. 'Well, right now, James, probably Barclays Bank.' And as a headhunter, bingo, that's where I am going to go. You can ask yourself the same question if you need that salesperson for your new business: Where are they working? What are they doing at the moment?

Once you have defined the role you need, and thought about whether you already know the right person, and come up blank, ask yourself the next question: **Do I know somebody who does know that person?** Call a friend, say, 'I've come up with this idea. Here is the basic background, and I am trying to find somebody to fulfil this role for me. Who do you know who's in that space right now?' I have no doubt that within half a dozen phone calls you'll track them down. The six degrees of separation rule definitely applies here.

When you meet a potential partner to talk about the business, you don't need at that point to get into the detail of how much money is involved. They will always ask what they'll get out of it, of course. I never respond directly. Instead I say, 'Well, why don't we go and meet the buyer? Let's talk to the guy, take a look and see what we can get. I do understand where you're coming from. I appreciate that you'd like to know now. Obviously, if we come away with a really good order, we'll work something out.' I won't engage, because right now I don't know what's going to happen at the meeting. I have no idea. I don't yet know what margin I am going to make. So it could go against me. I could land a huge order and find I've given too much away to my new partner. It's much better to be positive and reassuring. I concentrate on, 'What do you think of the idea?' 'Oh, I think it's brilliant.' 'Do you think you could sell it?' 'Oh, yeah, absolutely.' 'Listen, don't worry, I'll definitely look after you. If we get something really meaningful then it will be great for both of us.'

If you can't convince somebody to work with you after one conversation, I wouldn't call them back. They get one crack at it. In that discussion they are either in or out. If they are really not that interested, I'm not interested in them. Find somebody else who *is* enthusiastic about your idea. If they are too hung up about the deal, want to know all the percentages upfront before they'll agree to help you, they're not right for what you want at this point. What you need is somebody who is really passionate about your product or service. Because that is what they've got to go out there and sell.

If you understand what each of the constituent parts of your particular business is, you can use that as a mental checklist. Go through the list and tick them off. **Who's going to do the selling? Who's going to manage and control the finances? Who's going to execute and deliver the product or service?** If you haven't got a complete set of ticks, you haven't got a business opportunity either.

Giving yourself an extra edge

Finding the person who has the right skills which you don't possess could have a dramatic impact on your chance of success. I was working with a supply chain management business that had been set up by someone whose background, like mine, was primarily in HR. The business was doing fine but seemed to have plateaued. We needed a radical shift in gears to move on from the status quo, so I suggested we find somebody who was a specialist, somebody who lived and breathed that sector. I used my network, talked to a lot of people, and somebody came up with the name of a guy who happened to work for one of our direct competitors.

I met him and immediately I could tell he was right. He spoke the right language. He had a passion for understanding how a supply chain management service could be fine-tuned, and maximized in terms of value, cost and delivery, because the sector was his home turf. Naturally my MD was cautious about bringing in somebody who might be perceived as a threat, but I said, 'Don't be afraid of him, embrace him, because he adds value. It doesn't make you better or worse, just different. You both have different skills.'

I convinced him to hire the guy, and within six months the business was transformed, because the new guy saw things we wouldn't have seen. Because the MD and I both came from an HR background, every time a client said, 'I want more of this,' our instinctive response was to chuck another body at it. The new guy's response was to think, *Hmm . . . we need to tweak the software*. The difference was we would have taken on a £35,000 salary overhead, and he would spend £500 on a software tweak. All of a sudden our margins shot up because we were winning more long-term contracts but not spending any more money, just using the technology more efficiently. You needed to be a technology guy to think like that. And of course the MD was ecstatic. Which proves you should never be intimidated by somebody who has different skills from yours.

Bev James, who founded the Entrepreneurs' Business Academy with me, sums up really well why you should understand the value of bringing in the skills you lack: 'It is not what you do well but what you don't do well that gives your competitors an edge.'

At the investment stage entrepreneurs will often use the logic that it is better – because it is cheaper – for them to do it on their own. They are thinking, *I'll only need to get £50,000 worth of investment, but if I have four people I might need £200,000.* But that's false logic. In those circumstances it is actually easier to raise the £200,000: the team of four poses far less risk to an investor, because all the components are in place.

How quickly will that four-person business get off the ground compared to one in which a single person is doing all the work – however good they might be – and then having to chase the invoices, collect the cash? After a few months the one-man band is both drained and lonely. Remember, I was there, when I started out in my windowless office with only myself for company. I know what it's like – it is a real chore. Compare that to hiring four really good people who start off as a team together. There's atmosphere, there's buzz, there's competition. The whole thing takes off much more quickly. It's a more attractive investment. I reckon my £200,000 is safer because I've got safety in numbers. I am more likely to lose the £50,000.

I am no different from any other investor. Investors want substance, not a little island on its own that's going to drift. The objective here is not to try and make setting up a business harder, it's to be smarter.

I had somebody come into the office and pitch me his idea for some serviced office space. When he'd finished the presentation I told him, 'David, I think it's a great idea. But who's going to sell it, who's going to do the finances, and who's physically going to execute the service? Because while I still think it's a great idea, I can't invest in it at the moment because I don't think it's a one-man proposition. I think you need a minimum of four people to create a team to provide the credibility that will make the business viable.'

He said, 'I appreciate that, James. Leave it with me.' He went away, called me a month later and said, 'I've been thinking about what you said and, to be honest, I think you're right. So I've found a guy who's the finance director of a serviced office company, I've met someone who is interested in becoming the operations director and I've got a sales director on board now. I'd like to come along and introduce them all to you.' He brought them all in for a meeting and I was really impressed. He had put together a highly experienced team, the components were in place, all very credible. On his own he was not a viable proposition; with his team of four he was immediately more bankable.

Earlier in the book I mentioned Alia, the young woman who approached me about setting up a specialist media recruitment consultancy. Alia knew that it was important for her to convince me that she could pull together a top-quality team to deliver what she was projecting. I would not, could not, back her on her own. With no further ado, she started trawling the sector using the available search engines and networks like LinkedIn to research who was out there and identified around forty people whose profile matched what she was looking for.

She approached the top performers, including one guy who had been billing £500,000 a year where he was working. By offering him an equity stake and the opportunity to become a partner with her in the business, she persuaded him to come on board when the business took off. He then recommended someone else who was billing at a similar level. That connection led to the third team member. Even without an investment at that point, Alia was able to demonstrate she could recruit an exceptional, high-performing team, who collectively had a quantifiable billing record of £1 million in the previous year.

Great, that was just what I wanted to hear from her. It gave me a lot of confidence in her ability to understand what was required, and who she needed around her. It was as good as having an order. She had changed the risk level substantially.

The main aim of Day 5 in our seven-day process is to recognize and accept the need for a team. And if you know the people and you can get them on board in the early stages, there is an added benefit, a shared bond with those early supporters. You all come in together and are aware that you're exploring this business idea together.

Managing people and the mysterious art of delegation

Managing people is a fundamental principle of business. It is not everybody's most natural skill. My wife, for example, is an artist. She spends a lot of time working on her own, alone with her art. Consequently she is not a particularly management-orientated person. If you placed her into an environment where she was suddenly managing twenty people, I am not sure it would necessarily bring out her personal strengths and skills.

As always, you need to have the awareness to be able to define your own skills. Ask yourself, 'Am I a manager? Is it me?' If the answer is no, go out and find somebody who is good at managing people. Especially if you are setting up a service business, because in those businesses people are critical since there is no tangible product.

As an entrepreneur you need to get used to handling some tough final decision-making. The buck, to coin a cliché, stops with you. This business is your business. But not everybody is used to taking tough decisions. They have been too busy letting their boss make decisions on their behalf and spending most of their career working extremely hard at making sure their backside is fully covered. And the reason they manage to get away with that is that their bosses let them . . .

I was carrying out an annual review with a manager in one of my companies. 'James,' she said, 'I am pulling my hair out. These people are driving me mad. Not one of them can think for themselves. Every day they're knocking on my door, asking me for this, to decide on that.' She was really venting.

I sat and listened to her and then said, 'When are you off on holiday, Debbie?' 'Next month.' 'And how long are you going to be off for?' 'Three weeks.' 'So you're sitting here telling me that your staff can't even make a decision about which paperclip to order, and yet, can I ask you a question? When you go off for those three weeks, what do you think is going to happen? Do you think the place is going to fall apart? Do you think nobody will answer the phone, that the wages won't get paid, that the business won't run?'

She said, 'I suppose it will be all right.' 'So what are you actually saying to me? I can tell you what the issue is. The issue is you make yourself too available, and you make it too easy for people not to make a decision by themselves. Human nature is such that why would they ever bother taking a decision if you are prepared to do it for them? That's a pain threshold they would rather not cross. Why do they want that responsibility if you are prepared to take it off them? I'll tell you, it's because when it goes wrong then it's your fault, not theirs. The problem in this instance is not them, it is you.'

So if you have happily been allowing someone higher up the line to take the responsibility off your shoulders, be ready when you start your own business to find everybody trying to offload it on to you.

Many entrepreneurs tell me that they are not very good at delegating. Now actually I am very good at delegating. So I ask them, 'What does delegating mean?' 'Oh, it means when you get somebody else to do something for you.' If that is their definition it's not surprising they're not good at delegating. Most people delegate poorly because they don't communicate thoroughly. The clearer the instruction, the more likely that the delegated task will be done correctly. **Whenever I communicate an instruction very clearly, surprisingly enough it gets done quite well. If I give a half-baked instruction, I get a half-baked action back.**

Let's take an example. Suppose I want you to manage one of my customers while I'm away for a couple of weeks, and I say, 'While I'm off, could you go and manage my customer?' How woolly is that? The chances are that you won't do a great job, and when I get back and find you have had lots of problems, I am going to tell myself, 'See, I knew I wasn't very good at delegating.' But delegation has nothing to do with it: problems like this arise through poor communication. So let's stop, rewind it all the way back to the beginning and say, 'What does it mean to manage my customer?'

Now suppose I say to you, 'OK, what I'd like you to do while I'm off is call Brian. Brian is a customer we have had for three years, and he normally buys fifty of these items every month. He loves them in blue and he always prefers to be called in the morning rather than the afternoon, because he plays golf in the afternoon. When you call him, make sure you ask him how Suzie his wife is, because that always makes him feel that we have a good relationship. We never charge Brian the standard retail price, we always give him an extra 6 per cent discount because he's been a loyal customer . . .' Now, if I told you that, you could manage Brian. The chances are you'd get the order I need while I am away.

Delegation simply means giving an instruction. You have to stop and ask yourself how good and how clear that instruction is. If you have the ability to be very clear and very thorough the chances are that people will be able to deal with your instruction very well, and your delegation will be successful. You only get out of delegation what you put into it. If your delegation comprises an unclear, one-line instruction, don't expect a lot back.

Looking after number one

While you are thinking about the people who will help you launch your business, don't forget to spend some time looking after one very important person in this whole process: *you*. As you are putting your business together, how hard are you going to push yourself? Determination, passion, dedication, a high pain threshold, all of these are invaluable.

The business, clearly, is only going to be as good as the time and effort you put into it. Now if in your first year of trading you decide you want to take six weeks' holiday, there's nothing wrong with that. Nobody's saying don't do it. But there is a consequence: six weeks is 12 per cent of the year, so you've taken 12 per cent of productivity out of the business. This isn't a 'Should I or shouldn't I?' question. But it is a choice you have to make. If you are happy to accept the consequences, take the holiday. If you are not, don't do it.

I think most entrepreneurs would rather not risk that 12 per cent. I never did, especially in the early years. You want to give your idea the very best chance of success. Which to me means wanting to put in 100 per cent, not 88 per cent.

Even so, make the most of the public holidays. Use the time off at Christmas or Easter, those long bank holiday weekends when the business is closed. Relax and recharge.

What a little time away can do is to give you a sense of perspective. When I go away on holiday, the break does not necessarily generate any new ideas, but it does provide me with some thinking time. Because when you are an entrepreneur and in business, the one thing you don't get is any downtime. Most entrepreneurs are up first thing in the morning, still up last thing at night, running round like headless chickens. Even with a team around you, you are still going to be involved in discussions about finance, reviewing sales figures, negotiating with suppliers. You may be sorting out the phones, ordering the stationery, on sales visits to customers. Your twelve-hour day – and probably more – is genuinely packed.

It's a shock. When you were working for somebody else you had a particular function to perform. Now you are trying to cover a dozen different functions and therefore you don't actually get a lot of downtime. You do your twelve hours, come home, and in the evening you need to spend time with your family, because you want to dedicate as much time to them as you can. At weekends you're taking the kids to football, dropping them off for a sleepover, running about all over the place, and on Sundays it's lunch with your mum and dad.

So when you do get a chance to have a weekend away, you will find that subconsciously you have a lot of things in the back of your mind that you are trying to wrestle with, problems that you have not yet resolved.

You toss and turn but you don't want to make a decision, and the reason you don't make a lot of these decisions and you keep delaying them is that because you're always doing things, you always have deadlines, and you've not set aside the amount of time that those decisions deserve.

So I find that when I'm on a beach, rather than sunbathing or reading a book, I've usually got a piece of paper and I'm doodling away, thinking about whether I should move offices, whether I should hire this new senior person, whether we should expand, whether we should come out of a particular product. We've got a line of fifteen products and three of them aren't selling – should we just can the three that aren't working?

Over time I have realized that I need that time out to help me make better decisions. So I try to get away at least once a month, every month, for two or three days. I have recognized the value of that time and that the best way possible for me to resolve problems is to be in the sunshine or near some calm water, so that my brain is perfectly positioned.

I want all those knotty issues to move from the back of my head to the front of my head, because at that moment in time I am in the best possible state of mind to take a tough decision and make a good judgement call. **I am telling myself that this decision is so important to me that I must get it right.** And to get it right I need to be in the right place to think clearly about the issue. Consequently I correlate decision-making to being away from my desk.

The principle is that you need to remove yourself from your regular environment, because that environment does not allow you the luxury of thinking clearly. You are too distracted. There are too many things crowding in on you, demanding attention. The minute you are out of that environment your brain begins to operate in a different mode.

You the entrepreneur need to recognize that you need that time. It could be a day every month. It could be time going fishing, a half-hour run at the weekend, two hours sitting on the train, or watching your kids play in the sandpit. It doesn't matter. But without that thinking space, the quality of your decision-making will be very poor. You will be making decisions on the run, and – surprise, surprise – they won't be that good, not because you don't have the ability to make those decisions, but because you're not giving them the consideration they need.

Keeping calm and collected

When most businesses start out they tend to revolve around you, whatever you are doing. You are the critical cog in the wheel. And unless your style, your approach, your personality, your attitude are attuned to the people around you, the thing never takes off in the first place. As the business evolves other components will come into play: a brand, a name, an office, premises, people. But in the beginning it is just you. And everything about it stems *from* you.

You need to strike a balance between caution and risk. Of course you will need to be very cost-conscious in any business at the beginning, because you won't have the luxury of a bottomless pit of finance and need to keep a careful eye on what you spend. Therefore your relationship skills and the ability to develop good-quality relationships with your business partners, your staff, your customers, the people with whom you do business, are paramount.

Many people assume that to be successful in business you have to pursue some kind of macho business model, leaving a certain amount of collateral damage in your wake. I don't believe in that. One of my father's deepest-held convictions was that in business your gain – however good it makes you feel in the short term – is someone else's loss. Don't squeeze the last drop out of the lemon, he used to say.

I don't think you need to project an abrasive, aggressive or aloof personality. A lot of people have told me that they are quite surprised by my demeanour and my success, because they imagine you have to be hard-edged and hard-nosed to get ahead. I disagree. I think you can be fair and still be just as successful.

Perhaps the answer is that you should be yourself. The persona I exhibited on *Dragons' Den* is not substantially different from who I am outside the studio. When I first went on the show, I didn't try to change. I could very easily have been tough and aggressive towards the entrepreneurs, really stripped them down. That would have been the obvious thing to do, but I didn't go down that path because I realized I am not an actor. I don't want to be like somebody else. I am happy to be who I am. And it was true that being who I am probably proved more successful than trying to be somebody else.

It is very easy to get emotional about your own business idea. Because business is one big emotion all the way through the journey. This early period is when you need to be at your most controlled if you are going to be successful. If you are too emotional you will never be a great negotiator, because the person you are negotiating with will be able to read you like a book. You should aim to be a bit calmer, more collected, so that you are in a slightly more balanced position.

I am quite weird because I don't have a temper, so I never lose it. According to my wife, it's my most irritating characteristic. I never rise to the bait. Sometimes, when I don't react in adverse circumstances, she wants to shake me and say, 'For God's sake, James, get angry.' But my stock reaction is 'How bad can it be?' **Whatever happens, whatever the issue is, how bad can it really be? Because most things are resolvable.**

At home or at work, what do you get wound up about? When I was growing up, if I ever accidentally knocked a cup over and it broke my dad would go ballistic. Why? If my daughter drops a glass and it smashes I swear I don't bat an eyelid. Because, even if it's part of an expensive set, how bad can it be? She's come home late at night. She's safe, so how bad can it be? I've negotiated a deal and I didn't quite get the margin I was hoping for. I've made money, so how bad can it be? One of my employees has left. No one's irreplaceable; how bad can it be?

At one stage Alexander Mann was doing really well, then the recession hit and all of a sudden our revenues collapsed. No matter how we tried to cut our costs, we couldn't cut them fast enough to manage. We were on the edge and, to make matters worse, a cheque for £65,000 we'd been expecting from one of our big customers didn't arrive.

The JC twist

You're waiting at Heathrow, you've got a big meeting in the Far East to get to. While you're waiting in the lounge you hear that the flight has been cancelled. Everyone around immediately shows a mixture of anger, frustration and panic. They go into doom-and-gloom mode: why has the flight been cancelled, why is this happening to me? I take a different approach. I know that what's done is done, there's no use worrying about it. So I call up American Express, say, 'Hi, I'm at Heathrow Airport. I was due to be on the 7.10 flight going to Hong Kong. It's just been cancelled. Could you have a quick look on the screen and tell me what the next connecting flight I can get is?' Usually the answer is something like, 'Actually, there is a flight leaving in 45 minutes but it's on another airline, and you'll have to go via Frankfurt.' 'Great, book me on that flight, charge my card and give me a refund on the cancelled flight.' Now I can relax and make my meeting, leaving behind the other passengers at the information counter pounding their fists in frustration. I am simply not going to get uptight about it.

My finance director was in a state of complete panic. My office was next to his and I could tell he had completely lost it: he was shouting and screaming. I went to see what was going on, and he groaned, 'The staff's wages are due in three days and we have no money to pay them. What the hell am I going to do?'

Now even I was starting to get stressed, but I didn't say so. Even though deep down inside my heart was pumping, I said, as calmly as possible, 'OK, show me the bank accounts, show me the outstanding debtors. Are there any other invoices due?' He said, 'Yes, there are, but they are too small to cover the entire wage bill. We need that £65,000, or at least a good chunk of it.' The problem was that the key person at the main client had gone away on holiday.

I said, 'Have we spoken to the bank?' 'Yes, but the bank won't give us an extension on our overdraft because our revenues have been tumbling month after month.' 'Is there any other way we could raise any money?' 'No, not that I can think of.' It was pretty grim.

I went back into my room and I closed the door. For an hour I sat staring at the debtors' ledger, the list of all the outstanding invoices, thinking to myself, *There has got to be an answer. How can I not pay wages? That is suicidal.* I called the client who owed us the £65,000. They said, 'It's not signed off. We have a very strict policy that we can't pay invoices unless they have been approved by the relevant person and unfortunately the finance director is not here and he was the person who signed off on the project.' I tried to explain to them the impact it would have on us, that we weren't a bank. 'Could you not even pay me on account, pay me part of it, pay me some of it?' They said they'd get back to me.

They didn't, so I chased them the next day, but still couldn't convince them to part with what they owed. I called the bank myself, but couldn't persuade them to cover the shortfall.

I then managed to speak to a lot of the other smaller debtors and I think we ended up collecting perhaps £18,000, but that still left us about £30,000 short of what we needed. Now I could meet a third of the wage bill, but that gave me another problem: which of the staff was I going to pay?

I went the opposite way to what everyone thought I would do, and decided to pay the junior staff because I felt that someone earning maybe £15,000 or £20,000 a year was probably completely dependent on that salary. Now I had to give the senior staff the bad news. It's amazing what happens when you simply tell the truth. I didn't need to make up some long-winded story, I just spoke to them absolutely truthfully. 'We have got a client who was supposed to pay us but hasn't. Here is the invoice, this is the problem: the guy's gone on holiday without authorizing it and he's due back next Wednesday. I've spoken to the chief executive myself and there is absolutely no doubt we'll get paid, so I am pretty confident that we will have the cheque next Wednesday.

'That means I can't pay your wages this Friday but I give you my word that I am personally going to be sitting in the client's office at eight o'clock on Wednesday morning and I will stay there until I get that cheque signed, so please bear with me.' And, astonishingly and thankfully, they said, 'That's fine, James.'

On Wednesday morning the client's finance director was shocked to find me waiting for him first thing as he returned from his holiday. I explained exactly what had happened. He was very apologetic, took me into his room, signed the purchase order, issued the cheque. I took it straight to the bank for express clearance and by Friday morning we had paid the senior staff's wages.

Clearly that was a close thing, but if I had panicked and mishandled the matter, rather than employing my 'How bad can it be?' principle, the business would probably have gone under.

The moral of the story is that for you as an entrepreneur, finding a way to remain calm is vital, because business is going to be stressful. The issues are going to be challenging. You are going to be faced with different dramas every day of the week, I guarantee.

As the leader and central cog of your own business you need to learn that anybody working with and for you is going to be looking to you for leadership and strength.

The quality of the people you choose to join you will be crucial in determining whether your business is workable. In answer to the question posed by this chapter – Have you put together the right team? – recognize your own strengths and weaknesses and bolster yourself by bringing in people with skills that will enhance your chances of success and kick-start your business; think about how to manage them, and make sure you do that properly by looking after yourself and your own well-being.

Stay calm, stay focused, work with the people around you, share the strain, find the solution. **Give yourself a chance, not a coronary.**

'The further you travel along this journey, the more self-critical you need to be. This is the time you need to look even harder for that one thing you might have forgotten that could mean your idea doesn't work. Then find the solution that will make it work.'

DAY 6:
WHAT HAVE I MISSED?

During every day of this journey I have been encouraging you to take stock of which stage you have reached in the process, and to determine whether or not it is the right decision to move along to the next one.

On Day 6 I want to take this up another gear, so that even if you really believe that you have ticked all the boxes so far, even if you have a real business idea that customers are genuinely going to want, one that you can secure an order for, with costings that work and a team in place to deliver it, today is the day to go back and double-check everything.

We are going to try to find out whether there is still a fatal flaw. Can you discover the one element that you might have missed, even though it has been staring you in the face all along?

Because by this point you will be getting close to approaching potential investors, and any serious investor will want to carry out due diligence on your idea, your proposal, your business plan.

There is an inherent danger here. The strength of your desire to get this business off the ground – that very passion, praiseworthy in its own right, that is driving you forward – comes with an inbuilt handicap: a selective blindness, the ability to ignore or disregard anything that threatens to scupper the whole project. Everybody suffers from it.

Don't be scared of finding a weakness

One of the most important principles in my business philosophy is that you should never be frightened of finding out what is wrong with your business idea. Acquiring that knowledge gives you power, the power to correct the error, to adjust the model and make your idea even more bankable.

I have learnt this from sometimes painful experience over the years, and I now don't fear making a mistake. I know that subconsciously no one wants to make a mistake, but I don't see it as the end of the world, whereas a lot of people are still paranoid about getting something wrong.

In 2006 I bought the failing sandwich chain Benjy's from Deloitte's, who were acting as administrators. I moved quickly, too quickly in hindsight. I took a phone call that Benjy's was available on a Monday, saw the management team on Tuesday, the administrators on Wednesday, the bank on Thursday and made an offer on Friday. I thought I knew enough about business to operate successfully in any sector but I realized the mistake soon enough. I should have stuck to my usual principles of careful evaluation. I threw in the towel after six months, but I am still glad of the experience: I learnt more through the collapse of Benjy's than I did in so many other businesses.

The problem is that the fear of getting things wrong stops people doing anything about the very weaknesses that threaten to drag their proposal down. Their development is stifled because they won't move forward, and they won't move forward because they are scared of getting it wrong. But if you reflect on life you'll find that **you always learn more from your mistakes than you do from your successes.** For some reason you take your successes in your stride, but if you analyse your failures, or why you did something wrong, inevitably you will learn from that and become a better and stronger person as a consequence.

That fear becomes even stronger as and when the prospect of getting the business off the ground, of turning it into reality, grows closer. Everything is starting to fall into place. You are on the verge of approaching the investors from whom you hope to secure the necessary funding. You can almost touch the reality of your new business. But the closer you get, the more frightening is the prospect of falling at the final fence.

However, sometimes that pressure, where you can see failure right in front of you, is precisely what it needs for you to come through. Question your decisions, have the courage to challenge your own ideas. Nobody intentionally starts a business to fail, but at the same time, if you don't try, you will never know. As long as you understand the risk, as long as you are confident that you know how to deal with the issue, then have a go.

And don't assume it is easy. An architect, a lawyer, a doctor or an accountant will have spent years studying and qualifying, and that is why they might be earning over £100,000 a year. As an entrepreneur the potential rewards are even higher, so the effort you must put in has to be commensurate.

> **The JC twist**
>
> When I watch snooker on TV, I admire the grit it takes for a player to take on a difficult pot in a deciding frame when the whole match depends on him taking that one chance. He can't play safe, because if he lets the other guy in, he's toast. It's a huge risk, but he knows that unless he raises his head above the parapet there and then he'll have lost the chance. If he pots the ball, he's won. If he doesn't, the match is over. It's that close. So he takes the risk, and I admire him for it, win or lose. But if he misses, I guarantee you the next day that player will practise the same shot a hundred times because it was the one that lost him the match and he'll resolve never to let that happen again. And perhaps the next time he faces that shot will be in the final of the World Championship, and he'll win. Embrace failure and grow stronger, and you may find it actually opens up the way forward.

I know this might all sound quite theoretical – although it is rooted in my personal experience – so let me give you a real-life example from within my own family.

Hanah's story

My daughter Hanah recently came up with an idea for a business. She had been looking at the charity sector and realized that most charities are set up by people who are driven by a cause they are really passionate about, whether it's poverty, AIDS in Africa or autism. Setting up a charity is no different from setting up any other organization, and whether that organization is commercial or not-for-profit is irrelevant, because the principles are exactly the same. A charitable organization still has 'customers' to whom it needs to deliver a service. The only difference is that the profits are ploughed back into the organization rather than distributed to shareholders.

Whether I am building a village in Pakistan or fighting child abuse, I have to register a company, I have to attract people, I have to hire people, I have to pay them a salary. Those people have to deliver a service which has to be quantified, and there is a cost of delivering that service. I have to raise funds and attract capital. I have to pitch to organizations and high net-worth individuals. And just like any other business there are debits and credits. If I haven't got enough money coming in and too much money going out, I go bust.

Unfortunately, the people who set up and run charities often don't operate them like businesses. It's not their skill set or their mindset. They don't like to think of their charity that way.

Hanah said, 'Dad, why don't we create a business that helps charitable organizations to run themselves more efficiently?

There are 170,000 charitable organizations in the UK. As a family we have a foundation with the objective of helping people who can't help themselves, so we would be indirectly helping thousands of people by making the charitable organizations more effective.' I liked it; the idea ticked all my boxes.

Hanah went off to research the sector, and to work out how we could measure effectiveness in charitable organizations, to understand the services they provide and how much those services cost. She looked at other businesses offering help to charities. She thought about how, if we were to offer that service, we would charge for it, as a subscription- or consultancy-based service.

We looked for somebody who really knew that whole space really well, by running an ad for £350 on an online job board, and we found an amazing candidate with a master's from LSE in humanitarian studies and extensive experience in the sector with some large international NGOs. We took her on as a consultant. I told her, 'Your objective is to tell us why you think this *won't* work,' and set a timescale of three months. Within eight weeks we made it fail. We found the deal breaker: the charitable organizations would simply not accept they had a problem. I sat in on the pitches to ten of the organizations – talking to the customer to get feedback – and they all said, 'It's a really good idea, but *we're* actually doing fine.' As soon as we mentioned the word 'business' they switched off. We couldn't change their mindset.

Hanah came to a meeting with me to present the final analysis and she was gutted, obviously, because she had been very excited about this new venture and working extremely hard on it. When she told me the research meant it was not going to work, she was surprised to see a big grin spread across my face. I was really happy. She said, 'Dad, I'm completely confused now. Here I am telling you, after only two months, that my idea's not going to work. I thought you would be frustrated and disappointed in me.'

I told her I felt exactly the opposite. 'I'm ecstatic. The research you've done has been fantastic. And thanks to the research I have just saved a month of costs and consultancy fees, and beyond that probably £500,000 worth of investment in a business that nine months down the line you would have found that nobody wanted to sign up to. So we have won.'

And in fact Hanah had discovered during her research that the government was promoting the concept of social entrepreneurship with a fund of £600 million allocated to invest in intermediaries that facilitate social enterprise in the UK. She said she had noticed a lot of people with great scalable, profitable ideas for social-impact businesses.

'The problem is they are quite creative and innovative individuals but they don't have a clue about how to take that creativity and that passion and turn it into a business proposition which they could take to an institution and raise funds. The people out there with the cash are rather faceless institutional funds who aren't attracting enough opportunities. They are sitting there with this pot of money but don't know where to find the people with great ideas, and we've got these people with these great ideas who haven't got the ability to structure the ideas.'

She now wanted to create a business to bring the two together, using the private equity skills already within Hamilton Bradshaw to take a social entrepreneur and lead him or her through the system so they could come out the other end being able to pitch the most immaculate presentation, and hook them up with the institutions.

I sat there thinking, *Wow, what a good idea*. While listening to her, I was trying to find the holes. And I couldn't. We had a new business opportunity. **From an apparent negative – a business idea that didn't work – came one that did.** And in that meeting with Hanah she had gone from being quite disillusioned to being once again incredibly motivated.

Exploring the sales journey

So what sort of problems can trip you up at this late stage?

One that I frequently encounter at the point when a business idea is apparently shaping up well is that entrepreneurs have not properly thought through how they are going to get their product or service to market.

You can have the best idea in the world – the mechanics are all in place, the numbers work, it makes a margin, you know that it's a bankable idea, all the projections show it is going to work – but it will still fail if you can't market it.

If somebody comes to me and pitches an idea, first of all I will give it the five-minute test. If, after five minutes, I get the idea and it sounds interesting, I ask, 'Where are you going to make it? How much is it going to cost?' Another five minutes, and I can cut out all the other detail. Because right now that other detail doesn't matter to me. My next question is going to be, 'How will you market it?' If they can't answer that question I've killed the idea there and then. **There are thousands of great ideas out there, but if the marketing plan is weak, they will always struggle to survive.**

At this point I'll usually hear something rather vague in response: 'I'm planning to get a PR firm involved . . . I'll hire a salesman.' That's not good enough. Unless you have worked out that you have a real angle, I wouldn't touch it. I need to hear specifics: 'I've spoken to this website' or 'I've tested it on social media. I've looked on Google Analytics and there's hardly anybody out there doing this. I've worked out what the cost of marketing will be. I've worked out what the pay per click is. They are telling me if I get this many clicks, it will turn a profit.'

Or I need to know they've spoken to a distributor who says that if they can deliver the product to him for a certain price he will take it on. I need to know they understand the issue. I need to know that they recognize the challenge.

So often it is the cost of getting the product or the service to market that prohibits you from making any money out of it. The finances are closely connected to this cost of acquisition of the customer. One of the biggest questions in business is, **'What does it actually cost you to generate the customer?'** If the cost is so great that the business loses money, it's not viable.

This is, of course, additional to the cost of your own time, which, as we already know, is one of the classic omissions in any costing or business plan.

I'll find this out as soon as I start to dig a little deeper. And because I know that 90 per cent of people won't yet have thought about these costs, which for me is a potential deal breaker, I try to enlighten them by getting them to tell me how far they have explored this: 'That sounds really good, tell me about that in some more detail. Talk me through the sales journey.'

'Well,' they say, 'I'm going to mailshot the customer, send him the information, and then follow it up with a call and arrange a meeting.' 'Do you think you're going to sell on the first meeting?' 'Probably not.' 'Do you think you're going to sell the second time you meet?' 'I'll probably get an order, and sign him up on the third.'

So it is a three-part sale. Typically a three-part sale could take you six to eight weeks. All of a sudden the timescale becomes an issue, because if it takes you six weeks to make a margin of maybe £100, that is not going to be enough to keep the business going. That is a fundamental issue, and why I want you to explore it in detail.

Finding the pot of gold

Again, let me give you a concrete example of why this is important.

I did exactly this, both figuratively and literally, when

I invested in Goldgenie, the company that goldplates and customizes iPhones, iPods and iPads, which I first came across on *Dragons' Den*.

I sat down with the founder, Laban Roomes. I asked him to take me through his sales journey. He said, 'I network, I call somebody, say, "Hi, Rob, how's it going? I'm in the business of goldplating mobile phones." Rob says, "That's great, how much does it cost?" I tell him £80. "Sounds good," says Rob, "I'd like to do that." So I go and see Rob and I can goldplate his phone in twenty minutes.'

'OK, Laban,' I said. 'So you are charging him £80 for this. Typically, how long does that take? You've got to find the customer, got to call him, make an appointment, travel to see him. However you decide to get there it will probably take you at least an hour. By the time you've got on a train, or taken the tube, or driven out there in your car and found somewhere to park, it's an hour, no question. Then you go in and see him, have a look at the phone, that's another forty minutes, because there is no way you are going to walk in there and not say, "Hello, how are you?" and have a bit of chat. Forty minutes minimum. You goldplate his phone. And then it's going to take you another hour to get back.

'In round numbers that's three hours. You are going to charge him £80, that's about £25 an hour. Now, how many hours are you going to work a week? Let's call it forty hours. Forty hours a week at £25 an hour, what is that: £1,000 in total? OK, let me be really generous with you and say you are going to work flat out every day – you are going to put in fifty hours solid, so you're going to make £1,250. Out of that, with the cost of materials, how much is left? That is your business model. And that means it is not a business, Laban. It's a lifestyle.'

The problem for me was that, having travelled up to see Laban in Enfield and discovered that there was really not much money in it for him, I knew it was unlikely there would be any money in the business for me. I was sitting there thinking, *Having come all the way out here, I need to find an answer because otherwise, frankly, I will have to can the deal.* Luckily I do this for a living, so instead of walking away I set about dissecting the sales journey.

'Number one,' I told him, 'we cannot operate a business that requires you to go to a customer. It doesn't work. The only way this business will work is if you market online. Somebody has to see your ad and think, *Actually, I wouldn't mind having my phone goldplated*, then place an order online, get a Jiffy bag, put the phone in the post to you and you send it back.

'*Now* it has a chance of working. Because now you can hire a young trainee and teach them how to do the goldplating. Hire them in for three days a week, let's say at £50 a day. Now, in one day, Laban, how many phones could somebody goldplate?' He said, 'Well, if it was me sitting in a workshop and I didn't have to travel out to visit clients, I could do thirty.' 'OK, that's already better, because now thirty times £80 in a day is significantly more money. You can even pay your trainee more, pay them £100 a day, add the postage on, and all-in that costs you £200, but you're now making nearly £2,500 a day, so you can afford those costs, and every day you will be making more than you are making in one week at the moment.'

Remember, Laban had been doing this for ten years. But **in those ten years he had never looked at his business model from that point of view**; he hadn't examined the cost of providing his service to the customer. Now, set out rationally, it all seems pretty obvious, but for ten years, he hadn't seen it.

The other critical point the story of Laban and Goldgenie illustrates is that by understanding the sales journey, I was able to understand how his business was capable of scale. For real business success, scale has to apply.

It was the same with Levi Roots and his Reggae Reggae sauce. For years Levi had been selling his sauce off a stall at the Notting Hill Carnival, clearing a few thousand pounds every August. That was his business. He comes onto *Dragons' Den*. Bingo, he gets into Sainsbury's. And now he's selling a million bottles a year. But the problem was he hadn't been able to step back and see how to take it to the next level.

Knowing your business inside out

Last year, out of the blue, a guy called Antony rang me with a business idea. 'Hello, James. You're Mr Recruitment. I'd like you to back me to set up my own recruitment business.' 'Great, tell me all about yourself, Antony.' It turned out he was in his late thirties, had been working in the recruitment business for ten years, had good experience, sounded the part. He ticked my boxes. So I asked him to come in to the office and tell me more about the business he was proposing.

He turned up and I asked him, 'What sector of the recruitment industry are you intending to go into, Antony?' He said, 'Legal. Lawyers make good money. They're all earning over £100,000 a year. We charge 25 per cent of the first year's salary, so we are talking an average figure per job of between £25,000 and £40,000.' That's good. I get it. I use lawyers all the time; they cost an arm and a leg. So I was really interested.

I called one of my finance guys and asked him to run me a cash-flow projection for this business. He joined the meeting and asked the same question I would have asked, the one I had asked Laban about Goldgenie: 'Talk us through the business, how long would it take you to make a sale?'

'Well,' replied Antony, 'once I have set up, it will take me three months to get up and running.' 'OK, but when you leave the company you're working for now, do you have any restrictive covenants?' 'Actually,' he said, 'yes, I do.' 'How long?' 'Six months.'

I interrupted at this point. 'So you can't talk to any of your contacts for six months? That means I am going to have to fund you for six months before you pick the phone up.' Already a question mark had been created in my mind. 'If you start with me in January you'll be sitting around for six months, only able to cold-call people you *don't* know, which is much harder than phoning your contacts.'

Then the finance guy asked Antony about his sales cycle.

'Well, I'm going to be calling prospective clients and I would plan to find the first good opportunity within two months. There's a certain amount of time involved in going out to find and pitch the candidate. I will find the candidate, pitch the candidate, organize the first interview, a second interview and with lawyers they always have to meet most of the partners – it's not just HR – but I would hope to secure the first offer within four months.'

'So it's taken you two months to get up and running, four months to get an offer. And when your client gets an offer, Antony, what's his notice period going to be?' 'For a decent lawyer, minimum three months, average six.'

I pursued the line of thought. 'So let's say he accepts the offer. He hands in his notice, call it four months. So we are now into two months plus four months plus another four months, if we're lucky. In ten months your candidate is going to start work. You'll then send in an invoice when he starts, and generally the law firm will take between thirty and sixty days to pay you.' Sending the invoice doesn't mean you're getting any cash in. The difference between cash and billings is worlds apart. **Cash flow is understanding your business well enough to know how to project it. Most people's 'projections' are no better than sticking a finger in the wind.**

I said to Antony, 'Now, tell me how much cash you are going to need. Whatever number you came into this meeting thinking you were going to ask me for, I can tell you that you are going to need five times that number. Because I am going to work on the assumption that you have no cash coming in for a whole year, during which time you need me to fund you, the overheads, the offices, everything.

'Maybe you will pick up a few deals from cold-calling, or maybe you will come across somebody who's out of work and doesn't have a notice period to work out, but that's kind of a risky assumption, because what happens if you don't? My advice is, if you do pick up something early, that's a bonus. But I don't think the business should be based on that. It's too risky.'

Of course my confidence in Antony was completely undermined. When he left, I thought to myself, *He just didn't think it through. He hasn't put in the think time. He doesn't even know his own business. He's not ready yet, in my opinion. He represents too high a risk for me.* So naturally I didn't back him.

Really understanding the sales journey, understanding the sensitivities of cash flow, that gives me confidence as a potential investor. Forget to analyse those elements and the deal's off. The vast majority of entrepreneurs never carry out that analysis. And that's why the vast majority of new business ideas never get off the ground. In fact, they never even make it to the departure gate.

Testing, testing, always testing

The whole objective in every single business situation I get involved in is that I am testing it and testing it until I find a reason that it *doesn't* work. And when I do, I don't just accept that, I challenge it. OK, that component doesn't work, so what could we do to make it work?

My attitude is that whenever I test any component of a business, I always want to test it with Mr or Ms Perfect. As the entrepreneur, you can't put 100 per cent into every task because you *are* the business.

If I want to test the sales journey I will test it with a top-notch salesperson, somebody who does that one component for a living and that's all they do, someone who has no interest in strategy, marketing or finance, who's not being distracted by the premises, the VAT, the phone bill.

The person I choose – let's call him Craig – is not an inventor. He's not an accountant. He is someone who looks the part, sounds the part, can pitch eloquently. All Craig is interested in doing is picking up the phone and going out to sell. He loves to make a sale. That is his entire motivation, what drives him every day of his working life. He is a real terrier. If I put somebody like Craig on the case I will know whether the sales journey works or not. Because if after the first three months he has spoken to a hundred people and hasn't got a sale, then I am going to think to myself, *This doesn't work*. I am going to be concerned because he is a specialist.

I will tackle it from a different angle. So we've started off with Method A, which is to go out and talk directly to potential customers. That's fine. But now Craig has been at it for three months and has only found two firm sales. 'I can't believe this. I thought we had a winning formula.' Maybe that's not the only way of winning a customer.

What that actually means is that this particular methodology hasn't worked. It doesn't mean the product doesn't work. It doesn't mean nobody will buy. What it means is that direct face-to-face selling to a customer isn't working. So, what about viral marketing? What about Twitter? What about Facebook or Google AdWords? Why not pay Google to send you every lead where somebody taps in the words of whatever you are selling, whether that's roller blinds, spicy sauce or goldplated phones . . .

One method alone is never going to be foolproof. So unless you do all of the above you are not there yet. It's only when you say, 'We have tried social media, we have tried direct mail, we have tried telesales. Craig has been out doing face-to-face selling, he has been out on the road.' If you have tried all of the above and nobody buys, then there is one very clear message: nobody is interested. You have got it wrong. But right now you are too early in the game.

But even then I don't simply accept it. I ask, 'Why didn't it work? What were the three key things the customers all said?' The answer comes back: 'The delivery time is too long. It needs to be lighter. Make it cheaper.' 'How much would I need to reduce the price in order for them to buy it?' Craig will say, 'I think it's about 20 per cent too expensive.' 'And what does the delivery time need to be to make it work?' 'It's got to be two to three weeks, not six to eight weeks.' I would then say, 'Go back to ten of the most promising customers you met, and ask them this question: "If I could deliver this to you 30 per cent lighter, reduce the delivery time to three weeks and improve the cost by 20 per cent, how many would you buy?"'

Only then, if he comes back after having those meetings and he still hasn't got any orders, would I finally kill it. Because now even if I were to do everything that the customers had asked for, it still wouldn't work.

But maybe Craig comes back and says, 'I've had one of the guys say he'll take a thousand if we do all of that.' Now I've got the reason to invest more time. I can go back to the manufacturer with some clear targets. 'What do I need to do to make this much lighter? What other material is available that this could be made from? And if it was lighter could I reduce the price? And how could I do this in order to get the delivery time down?' To which he will say, 'You've got to hold stock.' Well, I don't mind holding stock if I know I am going to get orders.

Even at that point it doesn't mean I accept it. Because **I will test everything to the nth degree until I can make it fail**. But throughout the journey I am prepared to accept it could fail.

Use this Day 6 to look for the weaknesses. Think carefully about the sales journey. Make sure that you have thought through every aspect of your particular business and that you are as informed as you can be about the particular unique characteristics of the business model of the sector you are in. **Keep asking the questions, keep challenging the assumptions, keep looking sideways.** And if there is a weakness, you'll be amazed how often, just by asking those questions, a better solution will present itself.

'As an investor my objective is to understand risk. If I'm going to part with my cash, like anyone I want the highest return for the lowest risk. And the higher the risk, the less attractive the deal.'

DAY 7:
IS MY INVESTMENT
IN PLACE?

My objective throughout this book about starting your own business in seven days has been to bring you to this point: Day 7, when you have a viable, resilient, realistic and above all bankable business idea which will be in great shape for you to take out and pitch to potential investors.

Investors take calculated risks. They calculate the likelihood of losing their money, and the probability of getting it back, doubling it, multiplying it.

Risk is part of being an entrepreneur. But when I use the word 'risk' it's not about having a punt, or being a high-rolling gambler. Business isn't about taking risks, it's about minimizing them.

So when you start approaching investors, put yourself in their shoes, try to get inside their mindset. Understand that what they really want is to be able to clearly quantify the risk that you are asking them to take, so that they can make an informed, rational decision.

Do I even need an investment?

If you have some money from a redundancy pay-off, or an inheritance from a relative, you may decide you are going to fund your own business. That's fine, but remember that I opened the book by flagging up the danger that you could burn all that money very quickly indeed and see no return by the time it has all disappeared. **Do you really want to risk your pension pot or your life savings on a business idea that is so close to your heart that you may not be the most dispassionate person to finance it?**

There is a distinct advantage to bringing in outside money: the process of preparing an investment document forces you to address all the issues that have got you to this point. And it puts them through the filters of additional scrutiny and business experience provided by third parties who, however enthusiastic they may be about your idea, will never have the same intensity of burning passion as you do.

Now, if you have secured your first order or orders, or landed your first major client, you may not need an investment. Because if you have that order, even the bank would seriously consider giving you the money. Don't overlook the bank option – even though it is a challenging place to get money at the moment.

If you are going to get financing through a bank, remember that the bank's position is about how you are going to repay the loan, how you will finance the repayments, what security you can offer and how great a risk you represent.

Look at the proposal from their perspective rather than yours. Address their issues *before* you address your own. Without an element of security they will not lend you the money. What security can you provide? Is there a personal guarantee, some property or an asset to pledge against the risk? If you are prepared to do that, you should tell them upfront, because you will be starting off the discussion on a positive note. And if you can walk in and tell them that Toys R Us or Argos have already given you a firm order, then let me tell you, the bank will take a very different view.

Obviously if you can get the money from your bank, then you should take it from the bank all day long, because you don't have to give up any equity: you don't have to give them a share of your business. In the event you have won a firm order, go down the bank route first, because you only have to repay the loan and you retain a 100 per cent stake in your business. There is no downside – just don't default on the loan repayments, because if the bank is your sole source of money, they could suddenly ask for it back.

If you approach anyone else for the money you need to get your business off the ground, you are going to have to part with a certain amount of equity. Of course, that may be worth doing simply for the fact that, in return, you acquire not only the cash to start your business but also somebody to share this journey, which is going to become even more challenging and demanding once you press the button. When you go to a professional investor you are also gaining access to their expertise, their network of contacts, their infrastructure, their business background.

But again, having an order in place makes a huge difference. If you go to the investors and you don't have an order, you'd give away a lot more. Let's say you might end up giving them a 50 per cent stake. If you have a firm order you might only give them 20 per cent, because you need their money less: you have an order that will generate cash for the business once you complete it. And the very fact you have an order in the bag is going to make it significantly more likely that the investors will have the confidence to back you, because you have lowered the level of their risk. You've proved you can deliver what your shiny new proposal is promising.

Preparing your pitch

As an entrepreneur and venture capitalist, raising finance is a business situation I come across most days of my working life. One of my mantras in any aspect of business is 'Prepare, prepare, prepare' – preparation is vital, whether you're going for a job interview, having a review meeting with a long-time client or walking in to pitch a business idea to me.

An ill-prepared presentation is unlikely to succeed in raising money, yet an extraordinary number of people fail to do their homework first. It doesn't make them look good, but more significantly their whole plan is undermined by their lack of knowledge of the fundamentals involved.

Even when someone hasn't produced a business plan, I can still usually get to the bottom of their business idea in thirty minutes, one hour maximum. Now it won't be exact, but the key message here is that it doesn't *need* to be exact. They tell me the basic idea. 'OK, I understand what you are saying, just amuse me for a second.' I reach over, grab a piece of paper and say, 'You said you are going to hire Deborah, what's she going to do in Month 1, 2, 3, 4?' They'll give me some numbers. 'OK, now using a rule of thumb, based on your particular business model, what do you think the rent's going to be?' And although they haven't brought a business plan along with them, amazingly, when I ask those questions, 90 per cent of the people I speak to know the answers. They have usually been working in the particular industry sector, or they've already spent months fiddling about with the costs of the components.

That's my attitude to the overall plan. Don't get bogged down. Keep your workings simple. Do them on a side of A4 in pencil, so that when you wake up the next morning and think, *What about the Microsoft licences?* or *I didn't include the web-hosting costs,* you can go back to your sheet and add a new column.

But there's no need to agonize over the micro costs. You don't really need to come back and say, 'Oh, James, I forgot to put in that we're going to give Deborah a mobile phone.' Well, how much is a mobile phone: £30 a month? **If your business is hingeing on £30 a month, believe me, it's not a viable business.** By all means put it in, but it doesn't make a difference.

Why don't we come at it from another point of view? In the vast majority of households, it's the woman who runs the finances. The household has a single or joint income, and it has outgoings. If you imagine the household as having a spreadsheet you'd have the monthly income which provides the revenue line, and then the costs: the weekly supermarket shop, school uniforms, clothes, holidays, a whole stack of outgoings.

It is the same principle as running a business, and I generally find that women understand business plans quicker, because they are used to running a household. Every now and then an unexpected expense arises – the washing machine breaks down, for example – and it becomes necessary to re-budget, because repairing the washing machine wasn't in your spreadsheet. It's the same way of thinking.

So there's an assumption that you know your figures. If you know them, why don't you just put the numbers down? An accountant doesn't know what your costs are, or what you'll be paying in rent, spending on the phone, or paying your staff. You are going to feed him all the data. He taps the numbers into a spreadsheet and out pops the answer at the other end. On the net there must be a hundred websites that will tell you how to write a business plan, and if there's anything you don't know I think you are better off researching it yourself, because this is your baby. You need to take ownership. If you don't know what the expenditure is, you are not ready to start a business. If you haven't worked out where the revenue is coming from, you are not ready. It's not an accountant's fault if you don't know those things.

Let's destroy the myth that you need to talk to your
accountant to write your budget. You don't. An investor
is not looking for a rainforest of spreadsheets. The
investors I know never say, 'I've got to have forty pages of
spreadsheets.' Like me they can very quickly work out what
the margins are from one page of numbers. As long as
you can use a calculator you can see what percentage of
turnover is profit, and what percentage of turnover is cost
base. Accountants naturally tend to over-complicate and
over-engineer. Remember we are talking about start-ups
here. We're not talking about IBM. We're not looking at
depreciation policy or amortization. And if you walk in to
see an accountant he is never going to tell you how much
revenue you are going to generate. How can he? He will
simply ask you to give him the information.

You can apply that 'do-it-yourself' attitude throughout the
setting up of a business. If you ask a lawyer or an accountant
to register a limited company for you, the charge will be around
£200. Alia, the young woman who was setting up her media
recruitment company, discovered that she could do it herself
online for a tenth of the price professionals would charge. She
used her own initiative in creating the commercial heads of
agreement document: rather than pay up to £1,000 going
through formal routes, Alia found a template to download
and used that. Most formal and legal documents are

boilerplate patterns which only need the specifics adding. It's a good example of not following the conventional route and challenging the predictable.

What I really want to know when you come and talk to me is that you have prepared the main costs, that you understand how your business and your industry sector works, and that – because you have read this book – you have built in all the necessary sensitivities, have taken into consideration those elements of holidays, seasonality, discount, stock and obsolescence.

Focus on the basics. How much money are you asking for and what will it be spent on? What is the cost base of the business likely to be – how much money is the business likely to spend on a monthly basis? When you look at that cost base over a twelve-month period, you will be able to produce an accumulated number, showing the peak cash requirement of the business. This is the minimum amount that you need to raise, or the amount that you will need to cover losses while the business is getting established.

You would be amazed how few people come to see me with that information. Already you'll have more than most other people start out with. Your costs are going to be pretty transparent and your revenue is going to be quite real. Investors like hard evidence, so try not to hide behind technical terms or unlikely future growth projections. You will have produced a business plan that is thorough, professional and demonstrates your understanding of each element and your ability to deliver and execute the plan. It is much better if you do this yourself rather than getting somebody else to do it on your behalf. Do it yourself and you will have ownership of, and control over, your business plan.

How much money do I need?

Many times, when people start a business, they don't know the level of funding they require. Working out what you need is an important and critical stage, and recognizing that is key.

Question number 1: How do you define how much you need? People generally go to one of two extremes. They either provide chapter and verse and spend months, and a fortune, producing the proposal, or they do nothing. In the first instance create a six-page executive summary, because you can do that quite quickly. If for the sake of argument your executive summary says that you are going to need half a million quid, you're probably not going to raise it. You could spend another three months carrying out the detailed analysis, trawling back through the spreadsheets and revising your initial estimate of £500,000 to £586,000 or £483,000. But that variation is not going to change whether or not you get the investment.

You need a reasonably accurate range to know whether it's going to work or not. If I thought the idea was great, it would work at £483,000, £500,000 or £586,000. **You have to have some real substance in the plan, but I don't need to know about the paperclips.**

You can use Google to estimate most costs: you will find

websites from which you can obtain a quote to rent an office or that contain salary surveys that will give you a good estimate of the cost to hire four people. The web has all you need to determine roughly what your costs are likely to be, and that's all you need: a realistic ballpark figure as to what it's going to cost to set your business up. And then we can ask whether, for what your business is, and what it is going to do, and how much it is going to make, your ballpark figure is correct.

Year 1 is critical. You put 80 per cent of the effort into Year 1, 10 per cent into Year 2, and 10 per cent into Year 3. Once you have a realistic Year 1, from there on you are simply adding some assumptions, which is why Year 2 is essentially Year 1 plus 10 per cent. Most business models will break even at the end of Year 1. If someone comes to me and says, 'I am going to lose money in Years 1, 2 and 3,' I am probably not going to invest. The risk is just too great. In most of the business propositions that I see, the peak cash outlay is in Year 1 – in Year 2 you generally start to see it generating revenue and covering its own costs. It doesn't mean you get the whole investment back, but by that time, having spent the money, you have now created an infrastructure and a business that is generating enough income by Month 13 to cover that cost base. And if it isn't, you have a bigger problem on your hands.

The basic rule is that if you write a plan that shows that you lose money in Year 2 and Year 3, my advice, however painful to accept at this late stage, is to declare yourself out, to get off the train. The chances are you aren't going to raise the money.

Making your pitch

When you make your pitch, do it with conviction and confidence. An effective pitch for me is one that places the investment opportunity in the context of the journey we have talked about throughout this book. For example, you could focus on the problem you first encountered and show why and how you came to develop the idea to solve that problem. Personally, if I can relate to the problem, and find it compelling enough, I am far more likely to want to invest.

Another key area of reassurance is meeting any key team members at the presentation. If you are working with somebody who is very passionate about the vision, they could handle the initial part of the presentation. If you have a strong financial guy, make sure he presents the numbers. There is absolutely nothing wrong in having two, three or four people making the presentation. You should sell your people to the investor during the presentation, since the credibility of the team is critical. **I believe 90 per cent of the decision is about backing the team, not the idea.**

With the right preparation and the support of your team, you will be in a good position to give sensible, realistic, considered and factually based responses to all the questions I am going to be asking you as I probe around and peer inside your business model. When I look at your business plan and say, 'This is ridiculous,' you can say, 'No, it's not, James. I've already got the first order and it's turning more of a profit than I've put in the plan.' Any potential investor is going to feel really comfortable because the deliverability of the plan is there.

Here is an important footnote: just as you would in preparing for a job interview, you should do your research on the investor or investors you are going to see. Check them out on Google, read any press coverage, any interviews where they have set out their business philosophy. Which other companies have they invested in? It is absolutely key to understand their backgrounds and their motivations. That will help you tailor your pitch and allow you to engage with them on a more personal level.

It sounds obvious to say you should have practised giving your presentation, but I've seen many pitches where the presenter clearly has *not* rehearsed. They flap about with too many pieces of paper, forget their train of thought, or rely too heavily on PowerPoint, simply regurgitating in an uninspiring monotone the information on each slide which I have read and absorbed almost as soon as it came up on screen.

I think your basic investment pitch should be no longer than three minutes, an executive summary of your idea that will hook in the investors. You don't need to lay out every single detail.

Don't drone through every fact, figure and intricacy contained in the business plan. The document, however good, however professional, is not in itself the determining factor. Potential investors will be able to study that in detail after you've gone. **The key influence in the pitch is your**

ability to communicate and inspire with your passion, your drive and your ability to execute the plan.
I want people to talk to me, look me in the eye, explain their motivation, make me understand why they are going to make that extra sacrifice.

Leave space for the investors to quiz you on the proposal. Invite questions. This will allow them to set out their own agenda, and give you a pretty good clue about the areas they are looking for reassurance on. If they say, 'That's interesting, now tell me about the margins,' you can answer that point specifically and directly, and that is the perfect moment to refer to your PowerPoint graphs or charts to illustrate the figures you give them.

Interact with them. Answer their questions realistically. If they want you to tell them what the downside for risk is, and you cheerfully say there is no downside, that is patently not going to be true. You risk looking like a fool, or at best very badly informed, and guess what, you won't be walking out of there with an investment.

One final point on pitching to investors: make sure you convey what it is about *you* that is crucial to the business. What commercial value do you personally bring to the proposal: is it your network of contacts, your understanding and experience in the sector, your track record in delivering and exceeding targets? Demonstrate and underline your personal added value, because otherwise anyone out there could run this business, and if that's the case, an investor is not going to be interested in your proposition.

How much equity should I be looking for?

As you start off, before you get the business going, you own 100 per cent of nothing, and **100 per cent of nothing is still worth nothing. So are you better off owning a smaller percentage of something that's going to work?**

A lot of entrepreneurs get hung up about equity. In *Dragons' Den*, when an investment is in the offing, there is often a moment where the entrepreneurs, who have come in offering 20 per cent of their business against a certain level of investment, are obliged to reconsider that because – not surprisingly – none of the Dragons are meekly going to roll over and give them everything they want. If there's more than one person pitching they head off for a huddle at the back of the set, whispering together and apparently weighing up the pros and cons of the different percentages. And I suspect that in virtually every case, they have very little idea what the real value of those percentages is. They'll come back and try to barter with the Dragons, but it is very rare that they can accurately calculate what is actually on offer, so the bartering is just for show, a bit of posturing to make them feel like smart cookies.

The reality is that only once in a blue moon does an entrepreneur in the Den turn down the final offer, because they desperately want the business to take off or expand, and they understand, perhaps without being able to articulate it, that being on the show is a two-way street. You are trading off the national TV exposure, the subsequent coverage, the opportunity to work in conjunction with a collection of Britain's top investors, and there is a premium that you are prepared to pay for that.

At a future stage, when a company is already established, there are more far-reaching consequences that might result from giving away equity, considerations to do with structure, shareholding, decision-making, board control. But when you have very little, giving equity away is less of an issue, because you are actually giving away a percentage of nothing.

What many people don't appreciate is that very few companies realize equity. By that I mean that your stake in the business is worth nothing until you sell the company, and how many owners do that? The answer is not as high as you think, probably as low as 10 per cent. In the other 90 per cent, shareholders never actually see a cheque. Hundreds of thousands of companies fail with zero equity.

If you own shares in a business there are two channels of income. One is dividend flow and the other is the exit value of the shares themselves. Again, what percentage of private companies pay out dividends? Not many. Small businesses tend to invest most of their cash back into the business. So when you have to give away equity everybody gets a bit too obsessive about owning the equity and not diluting it.

The same applies if you are offering percentages in the business to key staff. You either keep 100 per cent of the equity, and hire average people on salaries, which is the norm, or you own 60 per cent of the equity and hire four exceptional people to whom you give 10 per cent equity each. Which is the better option? Company A: you own 100 per cent of the business and employ four average people who are on a salary and have no personal stake in it. Company B: you own only 60 per cent of the business but are in partnership with four exceptional people, and the reason you have exceptional partners is that you have been able to attract the best in the market by giving them a stake in the business, which to the individual is worth a lot. The people you will attract by offering a stake in the business will be far more effective as salaried employees. You put those two companies side by side and watch them perform, what do you think is going to happen? The company with four exceptional people is going to forge ahead much faster than the one with four average people, and your 60 per cent of Company B will soon be the more valuable holding.

How about asking family and friends?

Approaching your family and friends is a perfectly valid option for raising the money. I would say that more than 50 per cent of small business start-ups use money lent by friends and family.

There is a very good reason for that. If you come and pitch me an idea, I don't know you from Adam. And as I've said before, ideas themselves are not that compelling, but people are. The one person who is more likely to understand you is somebody who knows you already. And that is why friends and family back each other. Because they have an edge. They know the person better than the investor does. All the investor has is a pitch and a plan.

Let's go back to the Power of Why from the very beginning of this journey. Friends and family know the Why? question better than an investor does. Because they know your history. They have watched you grow up or seen the way you operate at work or have admired the way you handled yourself during a difficult situation. They have seen at first hand the kind of person you really are. The investor doesn't know that.

When I backed my own sister Nazima in a business making samosas, it wasn't simply because I knew she had a great product – tasting them at her house had prompted the suggestion she should start selling them – but because I knew *her*. I knew how far she would go. I knew what her buttons were and I knew this kid would hang on for dear life before she quit. Which is precisely what I want to know as an investor. I want to know that she's not going to take my money with the attitude, 'I'll have a go and if it doesn't work, well, you've lost your money.' Generally people won't do that to friends and family. They *will* swim the second mile. The relationship between friends and family to me is a good one.

When I was encouraging Nazima to set up the business, she resisted. She said she wasn't a businesswoman. I pointed out that it was just like running a household but on a different scale. Then she said she didn't have the money to do it. 'Well,' I said, 'I happen to be in the venture capital business, so what happens if I put up the capital?' She said, 'Oh, no, no, I couldn't take it from you.' 'Why?' 'Because if I lost the money I couldn't live with myself.'

I understood that. 'Your fear is that you are going to lose my money and I am going to be really upset. Let's just imagine I wouldn't be that upset; I sometimes lose it on *Dragons' Den*, why shouldn't I lose it on your business? Let's say I am going to loan you the capital, and if at the end you succeed, give me a bonus – give me some samosas, for the rest of my life! If it doesn't succeed I will have lost my money, but that would be my mistake rather than yours. So just look at me, look into my eyes. I am telling you, I am OK losing the money.' And finally she relented! She set up the business and it did really well. And I'm still enjoying those samosas . . .

Of course you could lose your aunt's, your sister's or your next-door neighbour's money, but you could make them a fortune too. The returns are potentially amazing. When Anita Roddick started Body Shop, she had trouble getting funding to open her second outlet. Her bank manager refused her a loan, so she turned to Ian McGlynn, an eccentric used-car salesman. He dug deep into his savings to lend her £4,000 in return for a 22 per cent share in her business. It turned out to be a great move for both of them. Ian McGlynn sold his shares in Body Shop in 2006 for £146 million, making him at the time Britain's 165th richest person. It can happen; it does happen.

So I think you should ask both questions and not just one. It's a question of balancing risk against return. Yes, there's a chance you might lose your aunt's money (risk), but you might also increase her money tenfold (return). And if there is a potential tenfold return, then so long as you have a better than 1 in 10 chance of success, your aunt is getting a good deal.

And the truth of the matter is that friends and family know that they might never see their money again. They know, because the mere fact you are asking them indicates that they are the investors of last resort. When I was starting out, my father would have been the final person I'd have gone to, though fortunately for me I didn't need to get that far. Most people go to friends and family at the end rather than the beginning, and that is for obvious reasons. Because, let's be honest, as human beings we would rather lose money that belongs to somebody we don't know than somebody who is dear to us.

Nonetheless, you should take some time to think through the implications of losing money lent by friends or family, even if they tell you they are happy to invest and seem fully aware of the risks. They are investing because they love you and they want to see you succeed. If they do invest and in the end the business doesn't work, then you will naturally experience guilt because you have let down the people you love and trust most. You've taken their money, spent it all, and can't pay it back. **<u>Are your family ties and your friendships strong enough to survive losing their money?</u>**

Remember Alia, the young entrepreneur with an idea for a recruitment company, who jumped through every hoop I put in her way with grit, determination and then some? As one of the final negatives I gave her to address I said, 'Alia, the only thing I am concerned about is that unless you invest some of your own money, I don't think it's going to work, because I am not going to take the whole risk myself.' I asked her to work out how much it would cost to set up the business. She came back to me and said, '£250,000.'

'Do you have money to put in the business?' 'No.' 'How are you going to raise the funds, then?'

She said, 'I'll speak to my brother.' 'Oh. Why would your brother back you?' 'Because he really believes in me.' 'So he's willing to risk his own money for you his younger sister,' I said. 'Where's *he* going to get the money from?' She told me her brother had both his own capital and a substantial equity in his house. 'And is he married? Does he have kids?' 'Yes.' 'And he's prepared to do that?' 'Yes.'

I said, 'Alia, before you commit, please go and talk to him and make sure he is 100 per cent comfortable, and if necessary I might want to speak to him myself.' A week later she sent me an e-mail. She had spoken to her brother, he'd spoken to his bank, and they were happy to release the funds required for me to invest in the business. 'Here's his number,' she'd written. 'I've asked him to expect a call from you.'

I almost didn't need to place the call. Because to me the very fact that her brother was putting himself on the line and giving her the money she needed meant that he was saying, 'I believe in Alia.' And she was already saying, 'I believe in myself.' That alone was fundamental in my thinking. The fact that somebody who knew her better than almost anybody else, and certainly better than me, would take a risk on her, spoke volumes.

The JC twist

If and when you do go to a professional investor, what you have to remember is that investors are not stupid. Anybody who can invest £20,000 or £50,000 into your business – barring the odd exceptions to the rule – will generally speaking be very smart. If they are professional investors they know this is high risk, which is why for £50,000 they want a big slug of equity. The bank would have given you the money for an interest rate of around 5 per cent and you would have kept all the equity. So the difference between the bank and the private equity investor or the venture capitalist or an angel is that the risk-averse bank is going to make 5 per cent on a 'safe' investment, whereas the risk-aware investor might make 500 per cent or lose his money or anything between. The difference between the bank's guaranteed 5 per cent and 500 per cent is called 'risk'.

Now, if you have reached out to ten or fifteen potential investors without success, my recommendation would be to stop at that point. Clearly you are being given a message. Don't exhaust the proposition.

Either (a) you are not communicating your proposition effectively, (b) you are not in a position where your proposition has traction, or (c) the business opportunity is not valid. Go back and talk to the people you've pitched to and ask them what it was about the idea that did not work for them. The feedback will be extremely valuable. You can re-evaluate, take stock and, if necessary – even here on Day 7 – recognize that this particular idea is not going to fly. Take a deep breath, get off the train and go out and start working on your next idea.

Should I think about trying to get on *Dragons' Den*?

If you want to put your idea out in front of some highly experienced investors, getting a spot on *Dragons' Den* is a great way to do so. You won't see my friendly face there any more but the current Dragons will give your business idea a thoroughly good workout.

And even if you don't get an investment, that could be the single spark that gets you going. Look at Trunki, the suitcases for kids. More people know about the company for the fact that they were turned down by the Dragons, yet succeeded anyway. So simply to appear on the show is almost certainly the best single piece of free PR an entrepreneur could ever secure.

If you have a business idea that you think is compelling, that has passed all the tests, has generated the right answer to all the questions I have posed in this book, then, yes, you absolutely should go on *Dragons' Den*, because if you get on the show, and you get televised, fantastic. To get six minutes on national television, with an audience of 4 million, how good is that? And then if you do persuade the Dragons to make an investment, great, you've had a double whammy.

And if you go on the show having read this book you will have the confidence of knowing that you have already crystallized the idea and qualified the business. So that rather than having a Dragon ripping you apart in front of those millions of viewers and being told that your idea is not a business, that it is a lifestyle or a hobby, you have the opportunity of being the one entrepreneur who's not going to get torn to shreds, a great opportunity of being the person who can walk back down the stairs with an investment in the bag.

The end point we are targeting for this journey of yours has the same output. My cheeky subtitle would be 'How to Get an Investment on *Dragons' Den*'! And who better than me to tell you?

At the end of these seven days, you should be in a position to make a serious, viable pitch to any investor for a business that you have properly validated. Most people build their business on sand. That's why the whole thing crashes down. By now you should have a great foundation, a sturdy platform to support your venture.

The train has arrived at your destination!

'Congratulations. You've made it. Your business is ready to roll. That initial germ of an idea is about to become a reality. And now the real challenge begins.'

THE FIRST HUNDRED DAYS

You are now seven days in. Even God had had a day off by now. But you are still fired by the passion that has been at the heart of your idea throughout. You are still fuelled by the determination that has kept you focused on asking all the right searching questions. And you are experiencing the relief and exhilaration of raising the necessary money to start your business.

Have a quick celebration – and really enjoy it – but then you'll want to get straight back to business. You will be feeling excited and keen to put all your plans into action as soon as possible. However, the world of business is not going to hang around waiting for you to get started. There is plenty of hard work and many challenges ahead. The journey is set for you to move into the next phase, from theory to reality. Don't be daunted: this is a great opportunity for you.

Putting the essentials in place

As you begin to implement your business plan, there will be a whole raft of specific administrative issues and details to deal with. If you are setting up a limited company, you will have to register the company and its directors. You will need to sort out your banking arrangements and investment agreements. You will probably be thinking about finding premises and dealing with landlords and leases. You might be getting ready to brief a design team on a logo or a website design company on what your site needs to achieve. You may need to start thinking about hiring staff, employee contracts, PAYE.

Those may suddenly seem incredibly prosaic tasks – and there are a lot of them to carry out – which by their very routine nature could dilute your overall passion and excitement. They don't need to. First of all, view them as the important mechanical elements that will enable you to achieve your ambitions.

And in any case, none of those tasks necessarily has to be done by you. This is the perfect point at which to engage with other people who can supply the advice and experience you need to help you get things done. Hire in the professionals as and when you need their support. The beauty is that in the first few days and weeks you may not even need to tackle some of them.

The journey so far has been to establish that your original idea is a bankable business. Up until now, working out the

Although this book is about creating a workable business in seven days, it is also technically possible to set up a company within a week, whether you are planning to operate as a sole trader, a partnership, a limited liability partnership or a limited company. For example, Companies House allows for same-day incorporation for an additional fee, but even on the standard service you could achieve the same result in seven working days. It's perfectly acceptable too and quite common for some businesses to start out as sole traders or ordinary partnerships where there are no registration or incorporation requirements.

As soon as you are formally set up you can begin trading: the tax arrangements can run in parallel. For example, not every business needs to be VAT registered in the first instance – only when turnover reaches a certain figure in any twelve-month period (£73,000 in 2011). And remember that online you will find sites with advice on completing the forms and standard templates that mean you can do all this without handing it all over to the lawyers.

tax structure of your business has been irrelevant because there was no business. Many entrepreneurs detour from taking the shortest possible route to this point as they allow themselves to become distracted by all the paraphernalia of setting up a company. But the journey of a business is made up of far more than the mechanics. **We have to recognize**

the value and the importance of the mechanics, but they are not what will make the difference between success or failure.

Keep focused on the job in hand. Make sure that in the first few weeks you are still sticking to the core questions you have already asked yourself. Don't become complacent because you are now up and running. In fact you should be asking yourself twice as many questions, double-checking every aspect as you go along.

Can I improve my orders? What feedback are my customers giving me? Am I staying focused on sales, because without sales there is no income and without income there is no business?

Can I bring in even stronger people to help me? Am I keeping a vigilant eye on all my costs? Are my people continuing to build in suitable sensitivities to the financial projections?

Could I make more money on my next deal? How is the cash flow, because that is what invariably brings down a company in its early days? Am I being complacent and making too many assumptions?

What can I do better?

These questions are all part of running any business, but they are particularly important in the first weeks, while the business takes its tentative early steps.

Getting the word out

If you are starting to see a flow of good orders and new clients coming in, you may feel motivated to let the rest of the world know about these early successes. But before you plunge into a spate of promotion and PR activity, make sure you actually have something significant and valuable to publicize.

After I had become involved with Motormouse, we were able to secure an order with British Airways, who committed to carrying the products on all their planes. Straightaway we had something to talk about. So we contacted the British Airways magazine and organized a double-page spread with a story along the lines of the Motormouse team coming into *Dragons' Den*, getting an investment, and as a result of the investment landing the order with BA. And it just so happens that Motormouse is one of the best-selling products on British Airways. That's a story.

But if all you have done is set up a business to manufacture a new Motormouse, you have to ask yourself why a journalist is going to be interested in that angle. The answer is that he or she won't be unless there is more to the story. There are thousands of business stories every day, about new entrepreneurs, existing businesses launching new products, companies buying each other, companies floating. And every single day there are a hundred business stories which are more than likely stronger and more newsworthy than yours.

The only reason that a journalist will want to write about

what you've done is if they can see something really newsworthy there. What is often surprising is that **the newsworthy story is not necessarily what you thought was the obvious one**. I'll give you an example. I've mentioned that my wife Aisha is an artist. She was recently staging an exhibition of her work at the Albemarle Gallery in Mayfair, a collection which she called *Elements of Nature*, based around the creation of the universe, the Big Bang, water, fire, earth and wind.

I was being interviewed by a journalist and telling him about the exhibition, talking about her work, showing him the brochure. 'You could write about it,' I suggested. And he asked me, 'James, why is there a story here?' I sat there looking at him. And I realized he was right. Where was the story?

He said, 'If I'm going to write a piece, what am I going to write: that Aisha Caan's got an exhibition in Mayfair? With respect, James, there are thousands of artists who are having exhibitions all over the country. Why is this particular one of any interest?'

He didn't want to waste his time or mine, so he thought about it for a moment and then said, 'I'll tell you where the story is. Look at what's happening around the world. The tsunami in Japan almost caused a nuclear disaster. Melting polar ice is putting millions at risk from flooding. The story is that Aisha recognizes the devastating effect that man is having on nature. As a result of what humanity is doing the world is being turned upside down and Aisha is encapsulating the effects on the world through art ... *Elements of Nature* focuses on mankind's intervention in nature. *There*'s the story.'

The lesson to me from that conversation is that PR is all about thinking outside the box, about identifying the angle. The story I've already mentioned about how Sammy French, a single parent with two children, started Fit Fur Life against the odds is actually far more interesting from a journalistic point of view than the dog treadmill she was selling. But would she have thought of that? No. Because to her there was no story in that aspect of what she was doing, it was simply the life she was actively getting on with.

However, when somebody from outside takes a look and asks where the angle is, they can see that here's a single parent with two kids, so why is she doing it? Because Sammy would like to support one of her daughters who's especially bright; she wants to give her a private education. It's the challenge, the drive of a single woman trying to do that. That is what sells the story. And the beauty of the story is that in any coverage about Sammy, what is the one image that is always used to illustrate the story? The treadmill . . .

I would say that most entrepreneurs make a massive mistake immediately after starting a business by saying, 'I've launched my service or my product, therefore I need to market it, I need to go to a PR firm.' Off they go to a PR company and what do you think the PR firm's going to say? 'Come on board.' Just like the patent lawyer will if you go along and ask him whether or not you need a patent for your product. 'Come on board. We're delighted to have you. We'll charge you a retainer of £3,000 a month, we'll run a twelve-month campaign for you. We'll do this and that PR.' It all sounds extremely plausible.

But do they ever say, 'And by the way, we will guarantee that we'll get you three pieces in the press every month'? No. Of course not. They can't offer any such guarantee. You run the risk that by the end of the eighth month, you've had one piece in your local newspaper which you could probably have placed yourself by phoning one of the journalists directly.

It's not because the PR agency is no good. They are doing exactly what you told them to do. But the problem is, there's no story. Interestingly enough, even I did that. When I set up Hamilton Bradshaw, I went to a PR firm, told them I'd like to get some PR, hired them, paid them a monthly retainer, and the PR we had received after six months was in two or three small trade magazines, a couple of articles which had absolutely no impact. It wasn't the PR company's fault, it was the lack of a decent story.

So if, after everything I have done and everything I have learnt, I still went down the same wrong track, what hope is there for somebody who has no experience of PR? You have to determine it for yourself. If you can work out that there is no angle, no story, that alone should tell you that you are not ready for PR. Wait until you have something solid.

With Laban Roomes and Goldgenie, the fact that he was goldplating mobile phones and iPods was fun, but in itself not really a story. Then we signed up with Elton John's AIDS Foundation, which holds events every year. We approached Elton and said, 'Why don't we goldplate an iPhone, inscribe it with the Elton John AIDS Foundation logo on the back and your signature, and put a collection of all of your songs on the iPhone?' Elton loved the idea. So Laban gets an investment from James Caan, as a result of which he signs up with Elton John, and Elton is now auctioning goldplated iPhones at his next AIDS Foundation event. Suddenly there were enough components for a great news story.

Managing expectations and the unexpected

Perhaps one of the most important things to know and understand in the first hundred days of your business – and well beyond – is that **even the best laid plans will inevitably go wrong**.

Perhaps the supplier who was supposed to deliver your product on a certain day fails to turn up. So you have had no deliveries and therefore you have had no sales. Or there's a Middle East crisis, fuel prices rocket and the cost of your merchandise has to rise because of the hike in transport costs. Maybe your top salesman has been headhunted by one of your competitors. He's now walked and taken half your clients with him, so your sales have plummeted. Or just as you start out, the worst thing that could possibly happen, happens: somebody brings out exactly the same product as you, for half the price. You didn't see that one coming. All of these things occur in business, every day, every week, every month.

The list is endless. If you want to find reasons why you might have a bad month, I could go on all day. But that's the nature of being in business. You have to keep your head, no matter what is thrown in your path. Remember the secret is to stay calm, and say to yourself, 'How bad can it be?'

And just as you have to learn that nothing is going to be easy from Day 1, you need to realize that your professional investors – if you have them – know that too. They are perfectly aware that they are taking a risk. So don't be afraid of communicating with them, because they don't expect you to come along every month and say, 'I'm on plan, I'm on target, I'm on budget.' In fact, if you do, they probably won't believe you. If your business model was that good and that secure, the bank would have given you the money. Just be honest and open and talk to them on a regular basis.

And if there is some bad news, as there inevitably will be at some point, don't try to bury it. People are always scared to deliver bad news. When you analyse that thought you will realize how ridiculous it is. Because the sheer nature of the investment invites bad news. I expect things not to work out the way you say. I don't expect every business plan to work because I know it doesn't. In fact I *expect* you to tell me bad news. The problem is you don't know that. You think that because I have invested in your business and you've given me a plan, then you must hit every target.

Well, in the perfect world you would. But there was a period over one winter when one of my businesses was going to deliver, according to their plan, £100,000 worth of sales. They had been delivering their sales targets for eleven months on the trot. But come January it snowed really badly. Half of the staff couldn't turn up for work. I knew before they even phoned me that their sales figures in January were going to be disastrous. So when they called up, not only was I expecting the bad news, I completely understood the reasons for it.

The smart entrepreneurs who work for me can't wait to deliver me bad news. It's the naïve ones who hide it from me. Why do I call the ones who tell me smart? Let's say one of my staff rings me and she says, 'James, the company has had a really bad month, the delivery was supposed to come in, but it hasn't turned up, what do you think we should do?' It is a very clever question.

All of a sudden it is no longer her problem. Because as soon as I find out, it now becomes *my* problem. How can I go back to her and give her a hard time once she's told me? Now I need to come up with some ideas and solutions too. Because if I don't, I've accepted the problem. That's human nature.

The minute I know about something, I am involved, and the minute I know I am involved, we have to solve this together. That's why I think those are the smart people. By telling me, they have halved their problem. Whereas the guy who doesn't tell me has to face the problem alone. If I don't even know about it, I have no responsibility at all, and it's all his fault. He's failed; he hasn't delivered.

If you have an investor, the principle you should adopt is to **be open, be transparent and share the problems**.

And if your investors are family and friends, fundamentally all you can do is take a similar approach: 'It's bad, the delivery didn't come in, but I'm dealing with it.' Because what you are doing is managing expectations. What I have learnt in business is that nobody likes surprises. People would much rather be forewarned.

This process will continue every month, because every month something different will happen. However, the things that happen are not always going to be problems. There will be a mixture of positive and negative events. You'll win more customers than you thought or you'll lose some unexpectedly. You'll hire somebody you have been trying to attract or he'll turn you down in favour of another job. Someone else may demand a higher salary than you wanted to pay, or she might settle for less than you expected. Prices go up, prices go down.

Each of the issues and each of the journeys that are part of setting up your own business demands a particular mindset, a thought process. And by now I hope I have given you the ability to understand how to think, and how to challenge yourself. And with that strength of mind you will be able to cope with whatever lies in your path.

What I can't tell you is that, even if you have demonstrated that your business is viable and bankable and doable, you are necessarily going to succeed. And remember, no matter how big you become, or how successful, the challenges continue.

Bon voyage

I admire you enormously for reaching this point, because I know how much determination, energy, fearlessness and concentration it takes to start a business. And even though I cannot promise you success – that is going to be entirely down to you and the decisions that you make – what I can promise you is that if you apply the lessons in this book you will have drastically cut the odds against you succeeding. **Whatever you do, while you're still on the train, enjoy the ride.**

IT REALLY DOES WORK!

As I began writing this book I was in the process of starting up a new business. I realized I hadn't created a business completely from scratch since I set up Hamilton Bradshaw in 2003. Since then, of course, I had been involved in years of private equity and venture-capital activity. I had been backing people, buying and re-energizing businesses, and investing in some of the *Dragons' Den* entrepreneurs, but I hadn't actually started a new business of my own.

So it seemed rather appropriate that a new business idea should come to me right at the point where I was developing the framework for *Start Your Business in 7 Days*, and I thought it would be good to talk you through the evolution of that idea, so that you could see exactly how I implemented everything that is contained in this book, and how my thought processes developed from an initial concept towards a new, viable business.

My business idea was quite simple: to help people

grow their own businesses, and grow them much faster than they could do by themselves. But the idea did not come to me fully formed. There was an evolution in my thinking, and it went something like this:

The seed of the new idea was planted when I was thinking about the nature of the private equity business. It occurred to me that maybe 85 per cent, probably more, of people who decide to start a business are working for somebody else at the time.

So let's say Tom works for a recruitment company as a consultant. He's actually very good at his job: last year Tom billed £400,000. As he relaxes one weekend, Tom reflects that his take-home pay was £100,000 that year, which means that the company made £300,000 profit out of him. 'Ah ha,' he says to himself, 'all I need is a desk, a phone and an office somewhere and I could do this on my own and keep all that money for myself.'

Tom decides to leave the company he's with and set up his own recruitment business. Now, in line with everything we've learnt in this book, Tom will be able to become a boutique agency. He's going to make a living. He'll make more money than he did when he was working for the other company, but he won't build a business. Why? Because Tom is essentially a salesman. If you strip his job as a recruitment consultant back down to its core, that is what he is and what he is good at being: a salesman.

But business isn't just about being able to sell. Who is going to handle the finances, plan the strategy, oversee hiring staff? Unless you can build the constituent components of a business, it isn't yet a business. But Tom has never done any of that before because all he's ever done is place people in jobs. Like most entrepreneurs, he has been responsible for only one component within a company.

The good news is that Tom actually does pretty well. In his first year he bills £350,000, takes out £80,000, and makes a £250,000 profit. I should grow this further, he decides, quite reasonably. He finds a bigger office, employs an external accountant, and hires four more people. That's good: plenty of people don't even reach this stage. Tom takes his company further on, all the way to £1 million turnover, and he is making £250,000 a year, but now he is stuck.

The business has come to life, but he can't take it to the next level, because taking it further requires a completely different skill set from the one he has. In the UK, there are over 280,000 small and medium enterprises, or SMEs. They are called that because they employ between twenty and forty people, and turn over between £1 million and £5 million, but they can't progress further because they have hit that natural ceiling.

To take a significant leap forward Tom needs to know how to build a business, how to build a brand. The next step is all about developing a strategy with customers, about customer concentration, value added, pricing, about attracting certain kinds of people to come and work for the company. He will need to look for individuals to join him who operate at a higher level than he has ever managed. Even if he brings in an MD or a chief executive, which in theory sounds quite interesting, how does Tom manage a chief executive? What objectives would he set? So for the time being Tom decides to stick with what he knows.

I realized that this was a critical moment in the growth of businesses – they could either plateau or they could push ahead.

I would say that 90 per cent of businesses in that same situation don't have the ability or the confidence to move on. They have a good business model that works, at which point a private equity company or a venture capitalist or an investor might come along, and say, 'I like this company: great business, great brand. I like Tom. It all works. It has customers. It's turning over £1 million a year, and Tom is making a good margin.'

From the venture capitalist's point of view, Tom has done the hard part. He came up with the idea, he established it and he did the grunt work. It's like a car: the first gear is the toughest. He's now off in first gear. I come along as an investor and ask him what he's making. 'A quarter of a million a year.' 'OK,' I say, 'I'll pay you four times earnings, and I'll take 50 per cent of the business.' We agree a deal and I invest in the business.

At Hamilton Bradshaw, as a private equity company, what is it I do now to improve the business? I add in all the constituent parts that are missing from Tom's company. I bring in a strategy specialist and a marketing and branding expert and before you know it, surprise, surprise, the business goes from £1 million to £2 million, then to £4 million and I make five or six times my money. Tom, of course, is happy because his 50 per cent is now worth a lot more than his 100 per cent of the company was worth before I took half.

Now I thought, *If I analyse what I am doing, I am spotting a business on its way up, taking a stake and bringing in all the necessary expertise – and I can do that because I already employ those experts at Hamilton Bradshaw. I have thirty investment managers here who between them specialize in every component part of a business.*

And **that is the moment at which my new business idea started to crystallize.** I was still freewheeling, still thinking through possibilities. I asked myself, 'Rather than a situation where I go in and buy a stake, why don't I approach businesses and say, "I will help you scale your business"? You don't have to sell to me because I don't want you to sell to me. I want you to keep the equity, but I have the expertise to teach you how to scale.

'I have a brand and I have an existing model. It's not theory. I can give you specific examples of ten businesses I picked up in the last five years and show you how well they are performing. Here's one that was making £2 million a year when I invested; it now makes £6 million. Here's someone who was making £100,000 a year; he's now making £1 million. I can demonstrate to you anywhere between double and triple to ten times the performance.'

That sounds a fairly convincing pitch. So then I asked myself, 'Would these companies buy that service? I think they would. Let's say I am going to charge them a retainer of a few thousand pounds a month, because there is a cost involved for me to put my experts in. For that retainer they will have access to specialists who can come in and unlock the potential of a business. For a company turning over £1 million to £3 million a year, could I convince them to spend just a four-figure sum each month? I think I could.'

My pitch for the retainer would be: 'I don't make any money out of that few thousand a month because by the time I pay the experts and my costs, there is no margin in it for me. So what I propose to you is: if I achieve what I say, I will take a percentage of the upside. In other words I want a share only of any additional value that I create. If I fail to add value, then it costs you nothing more than the retainer. If I succeed, then you've got a good percentage of something you would never otherwise have had.'

At this stage I talked to a couple of the team in the office and their view was, 'We can't think why it *wouldn't* work, because effectively that is what we do anyway.' I decided we should pitch some clients, because I didn't want to waste time designing a website and printing a brochure. I went straight to the market because I wanted somebody to tell me why it *wouldn't* work. We identified ten clients. We pitched ten clients. And two of them signed up. We had our first orders.

So I was now stuck on delivery. How would we deliver our service? Could we use the existing Hamilton Bradshaw staff? No, we couldn't really do that because the investment managers were already working flat out. We could have built our own business, but that would have been a big risk because each of these specialists was on six figures a year, plus NI, plus expenses.

We spent some time kicking ideas around, but I couldn't find the solution, the angle that was going to make it all work. Then, purely by chance, I found myself talking to a senior director in his early fifties who had worked for one of the large corporates for fifteen years.

He had since built and sold two successful businesses. His expertise was in sales, marketing and finance, and he was now looking for a non-executive-director type of position. He approached me and said, 'I understand you have all these businesses. I think I can add a lot of value and expertise to them. Is there some way in which I could get involved as I am looking to diversify my portfolio?'

As he was talking I was thinking, *Actually, yes you could. All day long. You're very good, you're very polished, well educated and, importantly, you have built and sold businesses before. You could walk into most businesses because the level of experience you have is much higher than the directors in an SME.*

I asked him, 'How do you market yourself? What do you do? Are you just cold-calling people?' Yes, he was. I said, 'It must be difficult because you have no brand. You're just on your own, pitching yourself.' Over the following few days I found myself thinking about him, and wondering how many more of him were out there. Because he was my man. He was the person who could unlock my business idea, make it deliverable.

I talked to three or four headhunting firms who specialized in non-executive positions. I called them up and invited them to come in. This was my research phase. 'How big is this market?' 'Well, thousands of people want to be non-execs,' they all said. And then one of them made a remark that really clicked with me. He said, 'When you get to that level, your dream job is to be a non-exec with five or six companies. You have a good portfolio, you take £3,000 a month per company. So if you can get five clients, that's £15,000 a month, £180,000 a year. Every month you go to a different company and sit on the board. Intellectually it is very stimulating. You're being stretched. You have the perfect job.'

Immediately I thought, *You're absolutely right. At that point in your life you don't want to carry on sitting behind a desk working for one client because you have been doing that for the last fifteen, twenty, thirty years. But if you can find five non-exec positions, that would be ideal. And clearly there are many people out there in precisely that situation.*

So rather than me employing these experts, why not create a business called Hamilton Bradshaw Venture Partners? I could approach this group of highly successful, potential non-exec directors with a straightforward proposal: 'Come on board with us and become a franchisee. I'll give you the brand, the name, the location, so you can be a Partner with Hamilton Bradshaw Venture Partners.

'I will share with you how to go in and create scale in a business, because that is what I know how to do. I will give you a business card with the Hamilton Bradshaw name on it, a calling card which means that when you pick up the phone now, you will get through the door. I am going to charge you to join for the franchise and I believe that with that you should be able to secure five clients at the level you would expect as a non-executive director.' It wasn't a bad proposition.

I decided to take the idea directly to the market-place. We ran an ad – 'Partners required for Hamilton Bradshaw' – and waited to see what happened. To my amazement we got a hundred responses. We filtered them out, brought fifteen people in, pitched the idea to them and we signed up three. Suddenly I was thinking, *My God, this works.*

My next question was, 'How many Partners could I sign up in a month?' I talked to a large range of people about the potential. I interviewed five or six franchise salespeople and explained the model. One of them was brilliant, twenty years in the business, a prolific franchise salesman. He told me he could sell three franchises a month. Great. Now I needed to find people who could introduce me to potential clients.

I had a meeting with one of the major high-street banks, and made a proposal. 'If I go to your SME clients, help them develop, grow, create scale, they will become better clients for you, because they will be bigger clients, they will be financially more stable, and they'll exit at some stage. Would you be able to invite some of your clients to a seminar where I can present my proposition?' The bank said, 'Absolutely. Because anything we can do to help our customers in this very difficult market environment makes us look good. We are bringing a proposition to them, branded with the James Caan name, and you're going to deliver a message that is going to help them.'

The bank selected 250 clients who fitted the bill. They wrote to all of them and 150 replied, saying they would love to attend. Now I had all these clients coming in who I could present to. Again I wondered who would be the right person to help me achieve this. I had met Matt Brittin, the chief executive of Google UK, so I rang him up. 'Look, Matt, we've got all these SMEs coming in for a seminar. I'd like you to come along and talk to them about the impact of technology on businesses and I'll talk to them about scaling their business.' We ran the seminar, and it went down extremely well.

I realized I now had a good business model shaping up. Banks and similar institutions were going to be my source of potential clients. We needed to organize a programme of events like the one Matt and I had just run. So I now needed to recruit somebody strong on marketing, branding and websites. I needed an event specialist to set up a series of seminars.

I already had one talented salesperson to find the Partners; now I needed another who would focus on sourcing the businesses who would buy the service. I was following the key message of 'Put together the right team', of understanding the key constituent parts of the business and making sure that I had people who were accountable and deliverable for just that one component.

I then ran through the numbers. We estimated we could sign up forty Partners per year. In three years we would have 120 Partners. We believed that each Partner should have at least five clients, two or three that over time he would develop himself, and another two or three attracted on his behalf through our branding and marketing. So, 120 Partners x 5 clients = 600 clients.

Our proposal was for the clients to commit to a relatively modest retainer per month, of which our Partner would keep a percentage. We were also going to charge the client business a small percentage of the value that we added to their business. We worked on the assumption that when we went in the client would be making £1 million a year profit, and over three to five years we'd take the company from £1 million to £3 million, so they would see a £2 million increase in performance.

We ran the numbers and they looked attractive over a three- to five-year period. Multiplied by the 600 clients we anticipated acquiring, that seemed like a seriously interesting commercial prospect.

Then I went to work on the sensitivities and built them into the numbers. I assumed that 10 per cent of the Partners wouldn't deliver, 10 per cent of the clients wouldn't make it, 10 per cent of the client companies would never realize their value, 10 per cent of the clients wouldn't reach the turnover we would expect. I ran every sensitivity you could think of: that the companies wouldn't grow, they'd fail, they'd drop off, we wouldn't sign as many clients as we anticipated, the Partners would fail. Even the worst-case scenario that was still rational and logical was looking very healthy.

Next I started testing the business for scale. If I had one salesman focusing on bringing in Partners, how much more could I do if I hired two, maybe four? I might do the same with clients. As with all business, I will keep pushing until it snaps.

But I wasn't going to anticipate it snapping before it even started. I might get to a sales team of ten and find that that is too many; if so I'll cut back to eight. But I'll still have more than my original one salesman. I will never be complacent.

By now I had taken an original idea and developed it to a viable, bankable model, and **what I did at every stage was exactly what I have been saying in this book**. By applying that mindset, the model was now ready to work.

And I could prove it worked. I had signed up the clients. I had signed up the Partners; they were buying franchises. The whole model was working. The new business was ready to roll.

We launched HBVP, Hamilton Bradshaw Venture Partners, in early 2011. By the autumn we had held eight networking events, seen the hits on the website mushroom in the first few months, established strategic alliances with companies including Google and Microsoft, signed up our first sixteen partners, and had deals in place with client companies from sectors as diverse as aircraft engineering, building and landscaping supply, and stockbroking. It was exceeding all my expectations.

I know not everyone is planning to operate in the private equity area. But whether you are thinking of opening a pasta bar or creating a new iPod accessory, the process is the same.

So trust me when I say that if you follow this seven-day approach, you are going to improve your chances of success significantly. **It really does work!**

A FINAL THOUGHT

There is something quite therapeutic in writing about what you do for a living. So much of the day is taken up with problems that need resolving immediately that there is very little space for reflection. And even though I am constantly asking myself questions about how I can improve both what I am doing personally and the businesses I am involved in, those questions are usually related to what is happening on a daily basis.

Stepping back and trying to articulate what I have learnt over the last thirty years has been intriguing and instructive. There were several 'Eureka!' moments, like the time I realized just how important and how powerful landing your first order was, how it moved the process along so immediately and so directly.

While I was reflecting on all the elements and determining factors that come into play whenever you are setting up a business, I was also fascinated by the fact that a number of new business ideas came to fruition during the writing of this book, each of which underlined the basic principles – including HBVP, Hamilton Bradshaw Venture Partners, and my daughter Hanah's charity venture. It was probably serendipity, but it seemed a good omen.

And I was delighted that Alia, who had come to me with her idea for a recruitment business specializing in media and creative jobs, and who had responded so well to every single one of my challenges and hurdles, got her company, Gemini Search, up and running in the summer of 2011. She turned out, as I suspected, to be a bit of a star. I introduced her to the rest of the Hamilton Bradshaw companies, and they were shocked that she had only been in business for a matter of weeks, because she seemed so far ahead in her thinking, and she had gone straight into achieving her billings target from Month 1.

The reason was that Alia had concentrated on the critical, core components of her new business. She had not been distracted by the non-essential nice-to-haves. And she had answered one of the key questions I had put to her: What is a recruitment business? She had recognized that a recruitment business is all about having the ability to attract people who bill fees, because that is your income, just the same as a legal firm – if you're setting up a law firm but you've got no lawyers, I don't really care what your brand is, I don't really care where your offices are. The fact that you have got the best software in the world is irrelevant if you have no one to generate fees.

Alia had gone out and put together a like-minded core

team who could deliver the business plan with her as well as consultants for their teams to deliver the billing needed. Only when that was secure did we look at all the other elements – yes, she needed some branding, we could get the brand sorted; she had to have a website, OK, we'll bring in a web developer; she'd need back office and accounting services, we put that all in place. And it felt so much better doing that when the essentials of the business model were already working, when there was a clear sense of purpose and achievement, and a team to deliver the business plan – so much more real to build a website and under 'Our People' list some genuine names!

Alia naturally felt fantastically excited about launching Gemini Search, after all that work, but she was also very confident, because she knew she had followed the crucial steps in setting up the business and that it was built on sound thinking and principles.

I am not a great fan of checklists and self-analytical grids in books on business, but here is the only one I am going to include in this book. It's a summary of thirty key points, and I hope it will be a useful reminder of the milestones you should be ticking off during your journey, so that you too can celebrate the launch of a great business.

1 Before you set out on the journey of starting your own business, ask yourself as honestly as you can whether or not you possess the DNA of an entrepreneur: do you have the inner blend of determination, hunger and fearlessness that you will need to succeed?

2 Understand your core motivation. Can you identify your personal 'Power of Why'? And is it strong enough to keep driving you forward through all the challenges you will inevitably encounter? Success is not just about the idea, it is about you.

3 Match your business idea to your personal strengths. Do you prefer working indoors or outdoors, alone or in a team, early in the morning or late at night, standing up or sitting down? Understanding those preferences – alongside your career experience – will define the idea you will feel passionate about.

4 The great upside of starting your own business is the thrill of freedom, the liberation from working for somebody else. You have been unleashed. You are now in control of your own destiny. That sense of freedom can be exhilarating, but it can also give you vertigo!

5 Your first idea does not have to be your final idea. Be strong enough to say 'I'm out' early on and move on to another idea that might be the one that works. You will save yourself so much time, money and stress.

6 Your idea does not have to be 'unique'. You don't have to change the world. The most successful business ideas are often simple, ingenious tweaks on an existing way of doing business, but delivering it faster, better, cheaper or more easily. You need to find your *compelling* selling point.

7 Establish whether your business idea is a hobby, a lifestyle or a scalable business and make sure you are comfortable with the category it falls into. I don't want you to be disappointed and frustrated by not becoming the next Bill Gates if your idea is actually a weekend hobby.

8 Don't be paranoid. Share your ideas. Tell as many people as you can. Ask for feedback and you'll be amazed what you can learn. Somebody will give you a piece of advice or the one angle you hadn't thought of that could make all the difference between success and failure.

9 Give your idea a tough grilling. Ask yourself if your idea is fulfilling a genuine customer need. Will somebody really want to buy your product or your service? And, if so, does the price you plan to offer it at match what they would expect to pay?

10 Research is absolutely fundamental to your ability to succeed. The information and knowledge you can acquire – from personal observation, detailed online research, going to networking events and talking to other people who are already in your business sector – is not just useful to know. It is *critical* to know.

11 Choose a name for your new product or service. With an identity, you can take ownership of it. Otherwise it is insubstantial, just a thought or a doodle. Having a name for your business brings it to life, helps you focus and starts the process of crystallizing an idea.

12 Concentrate on landing your first order as early as possible. Don't get distracted by all the peripherals of setting up websites, designing logos or choosing the office décor. Cut to the chase and find out if somebody is prepared to put down good money for what you are selling.

13 Use the power of technology to demonstrate a new product. You don't need to go to all the expense of creating a perfect physical prototype that might be unsaleable anyway. Get it mocked up as a visual or an animation. Remember how property developers are able to sell off-plan.

14 If a buyer is interested in what you are selling, listen carefully to what they tell about pricing, size, packaging, delivery times. They know their market inside out, far better than you. It's front-line research. Match your delivery and selling price to their requirements, not yours.

15 Sell with passion. That is not something you can fake. People buy people first. They like to buy from somebody they feel they can trust. So if you know you are not strong at selling – and you will feel stronger by admitting that – involve somebody who has that skill.

16 When it comes to costings, you don't have to be a master of the spreadsheet. Keep it as simple as possible. Work out the money that's coming in, the money going out, and what's left is your profit. If there is no profit, there is no business.

17 A few vital tips for your forecast. Don't cheat to create an artificial profit. Don't overestimate earnings or underestimate costs. Make sure you have built in the cost of your own time, and the sensitivities of seasonality, holidays, staff turnover and discounts. An investor will appreciate how smart you've been.

18 Apply the 'smell test'. What is the critical element in your particular business that is going to determine whether or not your costing is workable? What is the one thing that if it is wrong makes every other assumption irrelevant? Every business has one. You need to find it.

19 Make yourself more effective by bringing in a team of people who have the skills you don't possess, whether they're in finance, sales or logistics. This will lighten the burden on you and help you make much better decisions. Don't be frightened by their skills – embrace their difference.

20 Be prepared to take difficult decisions, because you are now the boss. Learn the supposedly mysterious art of delegation, which isn't about telling someone else to do something you don't want to do. It is simply communicating an instruction clearly with all the necessary information.

21 Look after number one. You are the cog at the heart of this machine. So take good care of yourself. You will be working extremely hard but don't push yourself into burn-out. Give yourself space to think, and room to be calm and collected even when the pressure is intense.

22 I don't believe that you need a hyper-aggressive business attitude to succeed. My father taught me that the best outcome of any deal for long-term gain was a win-win solution for both parties. 'Don't squeeze the last drop out of the lemon,' he used to say.

23 As you get close to approaching investors, be doubly vigilant. Don't let your passion blind you to any weaknesses in your proposal. You don't have to be ashamed of finding out you've made a mistake. I have made mistakes throughout my career. But I have always tried to learn from them.

24 Always take time to think about and talk through the sales journey. That is what often trips up a business idea right at the last moment. If you can't get your product or service to market, however brilliant it is, you will struggle to survive.

25 Never stop asking yourself whether you can do things better. Keep testing every aspect of your business to the nth degree, and challenge every one of your assumptions. The tougher you are on yourself now, the tougher your business will be out there in the real world.

26 When you approach investors, put yourself in their shoes. They want to minimize risk, so what can you deliver to reassure them: the security of firm orders and a great team in place. And don't get hung up on equity – 50 per cent of something is always better than 100 per cent of nothing.

27 For your presentation, the mantra is 'Prepare, prepare, prepare'. Do your homework, be comfortable with all the figures, know your business sector inside out. Keep it short, focused, professional but passionate: explain your personal motivations. Let the investors ask *you* questions so you find out the crucial element for them.

28 Going to family and friends for the money is always a route worth exploring. They know you far better than anybody else so they know how far you will go to make an idea work. Yes, they will be risking their money, but the return they see could equally be life-changing.

29 When you get your business off the ground, celebrate, then concentrate on making it work. Remember that your best laid plans will go wrong at some point, but you may also be surprised by what goes well. Be prepared to deal with the ups and the downs just the same.

30 Apply these lessons throughout the journey and you will have drastically improved the odds of your business becoming part of the 10 per cent that succeed. And when you have genuinely good news to tell the world, a massive order or a high-profile client, go out and let everybody know!

Acknowledgements

First and foremost, I would like to thank my wife Aisha, the first
'entrepreneur' I encountered, who taught me the true meaning
of the word. Thank you, darling, for being my inspiration for
the past thirty years.

I also want to thank my daughter Hanah, my 'guinea
pig', who throughout the past year has effortlessly and
enthusiastically tested the concepts in this book and who has
shown me that the journey is relevant not only to commercial
businesses, but to any successful venture, whether for financial
gain or not. Also my eldest daughter Jemma, who, as a result
of reading the book and believing in my own journey, has taken
the plunge and started her own business – Jasmine & Lilac –
of which I am truly proud. I wish you both every success for
the phenomenal careers you are undoubtedly carving out for
yourselves.

I would also like to thank all the people who have contrib-
uted to this book: Alia Majed of Gemini Search, Sammy French

of Fit Fur Life, Laban Roomes of Goldgenie, Patti and David Bailey of Motormouse and Bev James at the Entrepreneurs' Business Academy.

I would also like to thank Philip Dodd for his empathy and commitment in translating hours of my thoughts into a fantastic and, I hope, genuinely motivating read.

In addition, I would like to thank my dedicated team at Hamilton Bradshaw – all of whom in their individual ways continue to contribute significantly to my ongoing journey – with a special thank you to Deepak Jalan, Tristan Ramus, Nicki Shepherd, Liz Goldie, Jan Parker, Amelia Bamford, Stephen Mix and Faisal Butt.

I'd like to thank all the people involved in producing what I think is my best work so far. I hope this book encourages and inspires more people to embark on the immensely fulfilling challenge of starting their own business, and trust that it gives them the courage and freedom to achieve their dreams.

And, finally, my father, who continues to be my inspiration and mentor. In the early days of becoming an entrepreneur, his values, guidance and beliefs formed the foundations of my philosophy in business.

To everyone who reads and believes in this book, I wish you every success.

Appendix:
Using the Power of the Web

If you are starting out on the journey of setting up your own business, there are hundreds of useful websites available. They not only contain valuable advice but can also radically reduce the amount of time and money you could otherwise spend before you need to.

For entrepreneurial advice, the Business Start-Up Show (**www.bstartup.com**) contains specific advice and also gives details on the exhibitions, seminars and workshops they run.

I am involved with the Prince's Trust, which helps young people turn round their lives and supports their entrepreneurial activity. PRIME is another of Prince Charles's initiatives – a charity helping unemployed people aged over fifty get back into work by starting their own businesses. These three sites all contain useful information: Prince's Trust (**www.princes-trust.org.uk**), PRIME: The Prince's Initiative for Mature Enterprise (**www.primeinitiative.co.uk**) and the Prime Business Club (**www.primebusinessclub.com**).

Research is critical to understanding your market. Survey Monkey is a site which allows you to create your own free web-survey (**www.surveymonkey.com**).

The Entrepreneurs' Business Academy, which I set up with Bev James, offers training both online and through practical workshops (**www.the-eba.com**).

Mentorsme (**www.mentorsme.co.uk**) connects businesses with mentoring organizations.

For networking, as well as joining and using LinkedIn (**uk.linkedin.com**) you could visit Smarta (**www.smarta.com**), a support platform designed to connect business owners and entrepreneurs.

StartUp Britain (**www.startupbritain.org**) is a government-backed campaign by entrepreneurs for entrepreneurs, offering advice and support for start-up companies.

To find ballpark prices on setting up an office, including rents, look at Avanta (**www.avanta.co.uk**) or easyOffice (**www.easyoffice.co.uk**). For salary surveys to work out the cost of staff, XpertHR (**www.xperthr.co.uk**) and **jobs.ac.uk** contain salary surveys and checkers.

To incorporate your company online, there is advice on **www.businesslink.gov.uk** (which also contains advice on preparing a business plan).

Other websites offering resources and information for small businesses are **www.smallbusiness.co.uk**, **www.smeweb.com** and **www.newbusiness.co.uk**. Specializing in home businesses is **www.hb.com**.

You can follow breaking SME business news through

the *Financial Times*'s website (**www.ft.com/companies/ uksmallercompanies**).

Last, but definitely not least, I launched my first smartphone app in spring 2011. It is called James Caan Business Secrets, and was another way of bringing together my thirty years of business experience into one accessible guide, covering eight different categories, including 'Attracting Talent', 'Raising Finance', 'Marketing' and 'Leadership'. The app can be downloaded for free on Android and iTunes.

Websites for other associations, organizations and government departments which may be relevant to your new business idea and which you may want to explore include:

- Association of Chartered Certified Accountants (ACCA)
  www.accaglobal.com

- British Chambers of Commerce (BCC)
  www.britishchambers.org.uk
  www.thebusiness-startup.co.uk

- Chartered Accountants Ireland
  www.charteredaccountants.ie

- Companies House
  www.companieshouse.gov.uk
  Contact centre: +44 (0)303 1234 500

- Chartered Institute of Management Accountants (CIMA)
  www.cimaglobal.com

- Department for Business Innovation and Skills (BIS)
  www.bis.gov.uk

- Directgov public services
  www.direct.gov.uk

- Federation of Small Businesses
  www.fsb.org.uk

- Health and Safety Executive
  www.hse.gov.uk
  Ask an expert: 0845 3 450 055

- HM Revenue and Customs
  www.hmrc.gov.uk
  Newly self-employed helpline: 0845 915 4515
  New employer helpline: 0845 607 0143

- Institute of Chartered Accountants in England and Wales
  (ICAEW)
  www.icaewfirms.co.uk

- Institute of Chartered Accountants of Scotland (ICAS)
  www.icas.org.uk

- Investors in People
  www.investorsinpeople.co.uk

- Intellectual Property Office
  www.ipo.gov.uk
  Enquiries: 0845 9 500 505

- Law Society of England and Wales
  www.lawsociety.org.uk

- Law Society of Scotland
  www.lawscot.org.uk